Contents

Introduction

Chip carving as an art form has been around for thousands of years. The classic "chip carved" look—featuring precise groupings of geometric shapes set into a smooth surface—appears on grand cathedrals throughout Europe from the 12th century on. But the style has also adorned humbler, homier objects, from folk art toys to boxes and drinking vessels. These items were not simply decorative; they had an everyday function around the house. And they could be carved by newcomers to the craft, using just one or two simple tools.

In this spirit, we've gathered some of the best chip carving projects from our archive, including cereal bowls, barrettes, coffee spoons, holiday ornaments, and even a cribbage board. Each one is both elegant and practical—and many, such as Roman Chernikov's "Summery Supernova Coasters" (page 35), can be completed in just an afternoon. If this is your first time picking up a knife, don't worry—we've included tips and techniques from today's leading chip carvers, such as Wayne Barton, Marty Leenhouts, and Charlene Lynum, to guide you through your first cuts.

Happy carving!
The *Woodcarving Illustrated* team

About the Authors

Wayne Barton is credited with introducing chip carving to the United States. He was named Woodcarving Illustrated's Woodcarver of the Year in 2005. Wayne has written several books, and he teaches seminars around the country. For more information, visit his website at chipcarving.com.

Deanna Cadoret lives in Canada with a large family of animals. Besides chip carving, she loves working with yarn, drawing, and painting. Deanna has previously published a tutorial called Stone Wall—Watercolour over Pen and Ink on Wetcanvas.com under the screen name Kitaye.

Roman Chernikov is a software engineer who has been carving as a hobby since 2013. He lives near San Francisco and attends the Santa Clara Valley Carvers Club. For more of his work, visit readNtry.com.

Amy Costello is known for her delicate chip carving on turnings and small joinery projects. While she has built furniture in several industrial-sized shops since 2014, she currently does all of her woodworking on a 6' by 10' platform in her bedroom, with a long curtain splitting the room. When she's not in the shop, Amy enjoys illustrating, throwing pots, and playing Dungeons and Dragons. Find her on Instagram @amy.makes.everything.

Vernon DePauw started carving in seventh-grade shop class and has been carving for pleasure and profit ever since. For more of his work, visit his website at vldwoodcarver.com.

Andrew DiPace is originally from New York City, but now lives in Lancaster, Pa. A carver for nine years, he is a member of the Lancaster County Woodcarvers and serves as the club's show chairman, as well as a teacher of beginning carvers. He is also interested in bonsai, which often involves carving. E-mail him at LancCarvers@gmail.com.

Marty Leenhouts is a regular contributor to Woodcarving Illustrated. He has 30 years of teaching experience and is the owner of MyChipCarving.com and EZcarving.com. His videos have more than 2.5 million views, and he is the author of Chip Carving Essentials: A Step-by-Step Guide to Successful Chip Carving.

Charlene Lynum began chip carving around 1985. She lives near Eau Claire, Wis., and is a member of the West Wisconsin Woodcarvers Guild. What started as a hobby has turned, in the past few years, into an artistic adventure. Charlene appreciates the simple beauty that chip carving can add to a project. Find her on Instagram @thelynums.

Gary MacKay is a lifelong woodworker who embellishes his work with chip carving. He has been selling his wooden items at juried craft galleries for 22 years. E-mail him at glmackay@yahoo.com.

Paul Meisel and his team at Meisel Hardware Specialties have designed over 3,500 projects and plans for the home hobbyist woodworker. Dozens of projects from Paul's collection have appeared in Scroll Saw Woodworking & Crafts magazine. For more of his work, visit meiselwoodhobby.com.

Tom Noller started carving in 2009 after retiring as an engineer. He is the president and newsletter editor for the Lake Ray Hubbard Woodcarving Club, located in Rowlett, Texas. E-mail him at txwoodguy@gmail.com.

Steve Reed started carving more than 30 years ago while serving in the U.S. Air Force. An award-winning carver and competition judge, he has taught chip and figure carving for Midwest Woodworkers Inc. in Omaha, Neb. A member of the National Woodcarvers Association and Mid-America Woodcarvers Association, Steve lives in Bellevue, Neb. with his wife, Cathy. E-mail him at stevereed53@msn.com.

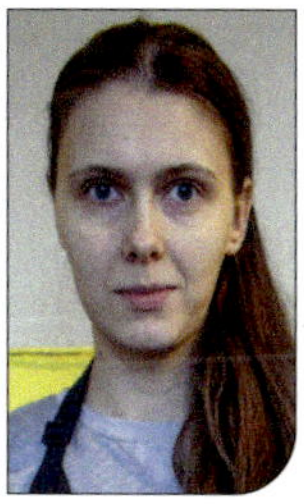

Roman and Olga Repikova have been carving for 12 years. Great lovers of music, they manufacture ukuleles and other handmade wooden items at their home in Ukraine. Contact them at woodcrafttt@gmail.com or on Etsy at WoodCarv.

Carver's Lapboard

Carve anywhere with this simple shop-made board

By Gary MacKay

When I first started chip carving, I would place a towel on my lap to catch the chips. With chip carving, you should have your thumb, knuckle, and knife point in contact with the wood you are carving. That's not normally possible when you carve the chips near the edge of the blank. To help support my hand while I carve these chips, I created a lapboard.

I made my lapboard with 1½" (3.8cm)-wide sides to allow plenty of surface contact when carving chips near the edges of my stock. The sides are the same thickness as the wood I normally carve and help to lock the blank in place. Additionally, the lapboard gives me a solid surface to carve on and I can sweep the chips into the drilled recesses to keep them out of the way while I work.

If you increase the height of the sides, you can use the lapboard to hold extra tools and catch wood chips when you work on any type of carving.

Step 1: Cut the sides to size. I chip carve mainly ⅜" (1cm)-thick wood, so my sides are ⅜" (1cm) thick by 1½" (3.8cm) wide. The length of the sides depends on the size of the lapboard you want to make.

Step 2: Cut the base to size. I made my lapboard 10" by 12" (25.4cm by 30.5cm), but you can size the board according to the scrap wood you have or what is most convenient for you.

Step 3: Drill the chip collection holes. Use the drawing to determine the position of the holes. I use a 1½" (3.8cm)-diameter Forstner bit to drill ¼" (6mm)-deep holes. *Alternatively, cut a piece of ¼" (6mm)-thick plywood to the size of the base and drill the holes with a spade bit. Glue the ¼" (6mm)-thick plywood to a ½" (1.3cm)-thick piece to get the ¾" (1.9cm)-thick base.*

Step 4: Assemble the lapboard. Glue and clamp the sides to the base.

Carver's Lapboard Measured Drawing

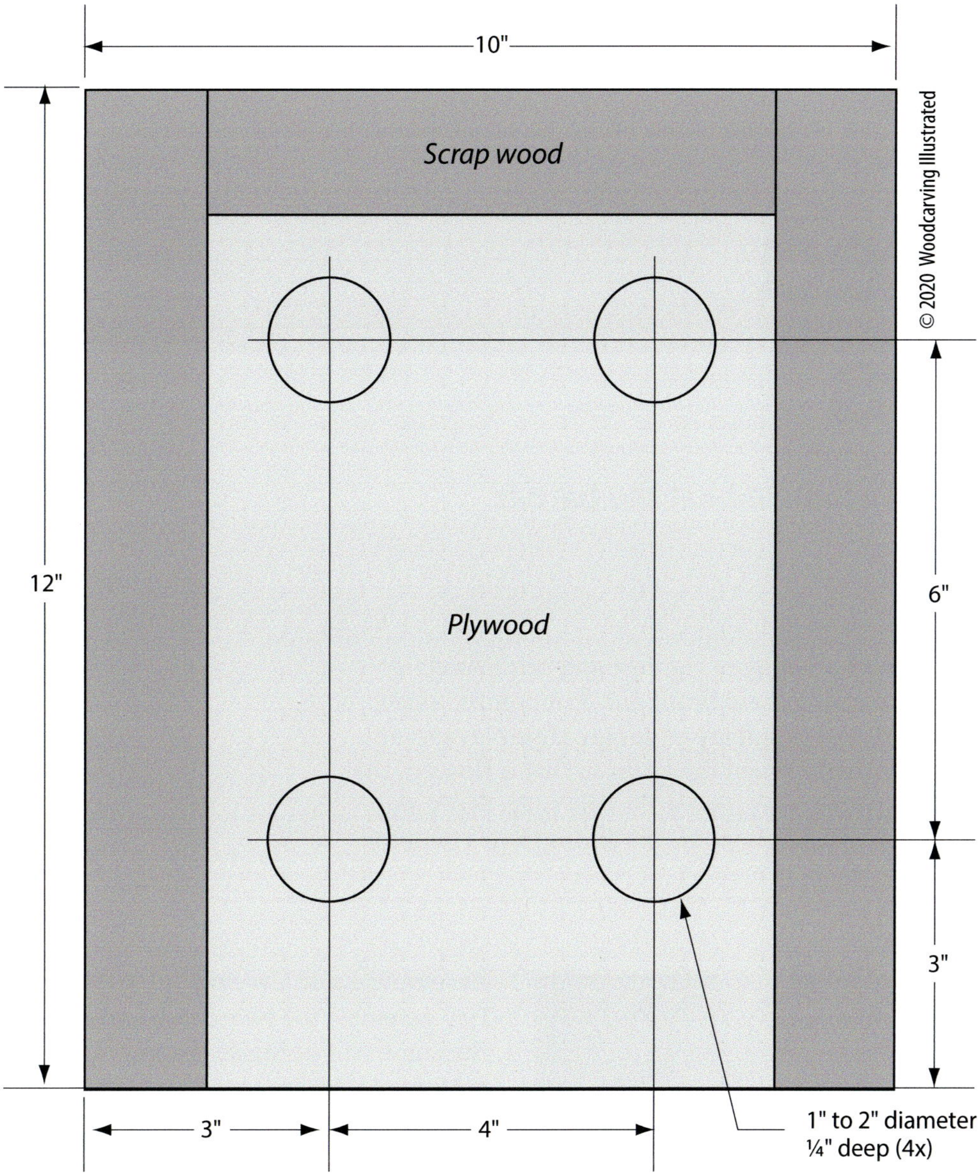

materials & **tools**

MATERIALS

- Plywood, ¾" (1.9cm) thick: 10" x 12" (25.4cm x 30.5cm), base
- Scrap wood, ⅜" (1cm) thick: 1½" x 12" (3.8cm x 30.5cm), long side
- Scrap wood ⅜" (1cm) thick: 1½" x 7" (3.8cm x 17.8cm), short side
- Wood glue

TOOLS

- Drill press with bit: 1½" (3.8cm)- to 2" (5.1cm)-dia. Forstner
- Clamps
- Chip carving knife

The author used these products for the project. Substitute your choice of brands, tools, and materials as desired.

Stylized Combs

Love your locks with a look to beat the barber

By Roman and Olga Repikova

Natural materials impart a feeling of comfort and bring us closer to the earth. When creating these beard and hair combs, follow two basic rules—practicality and simplicity of design. If you choose an attractive hardwood, make sure to orient the grain so that it flows in the same direction as the teeth; otherwise, they will easily snap. Stack and glue together multiple layers of ash veneer for the folding hair comb to ensure durability.

Getting Started

Sand down the wood pieces and cover them with blue painter's tape. Photocopy the patterns and attach them to the wood with spray adhesive. We use a CNC machine to cut out the comb blanks, but you can use a scroll saw with a #3 reverse-tooth blade. Drill the holes for the pivot pin in the folding comb and case pieces.

Assembling and Carving

Dry-assemble the hair comb and case to make sure the comb will fit inside the slot. Then glue the top and bottom of the case together, clamp, and let dry. Once dry, sand off any sharp corners.

Carve the beard comb and hair comb case. Start with the chip carving knife, referring to the patterns as you create two-, three-, and four-corner chips. Then use a ¼" (6mm) #5 gouge to carve the borders around the leaves and the perimeter of each design; use a ⅛" (3mm) #9 gouge for the feathering on the beard comb.

Sanding and Finishing

Once you've carved the beard comb and folding comb case, gently sand the combs to 220-grit so that, on a side view, the teeth taper almost to a point. Cover all of the pieces with walnut stain. Allow the stain to dry and then sand them again. This will remove the stain from the flat surfaces and allow it to remain in the carved chips, adding contrast to the finished combs.

Finish the combs with beeswax dissolved in turpentine oil; this gives them a beautiful shine and a unique aroma. Feel free to add a few drops of your preferred essential oil to the mixture for a personal touch. After coating the pieces, allow a little time for the wood to soak up the mixture, and then rub with a medium-to-coarse brush. Add the folding comb and pivot pin to the case.

A stylish comb to tame the wildest of beards and a folding hair comb perfect for storing in a purse or pack.

Stylized Comb Patterns

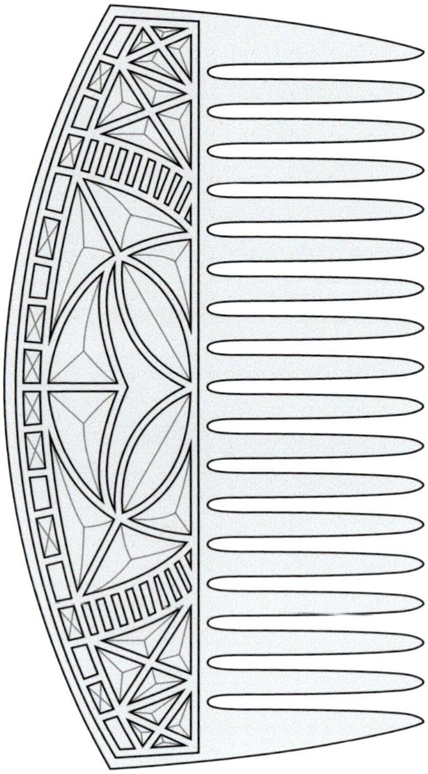

Homemade Knife

Roman designed this knife to carve geometric patterns and reliefs. It has a thin, sharp carbon steel blade, which is shaped to allow us to cut both toward and away from ourselves in a few fluid motions. It has a comfortable walnut handle finished with raw natural linseed oil, and works well for both soft and hard wood.

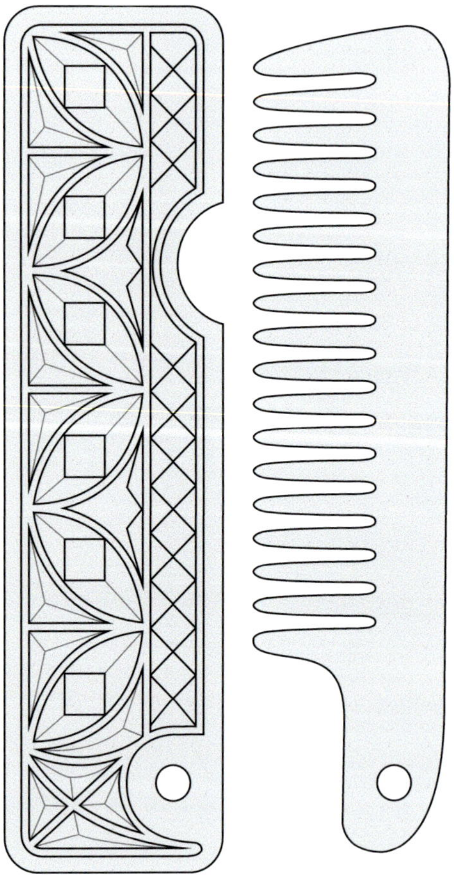

materials & **tools**

MATERIALS

- Walnut, ¼" (6mm) thick: beard comb, sized for pattern
- Alder, ⅜" (1cm) thick: folding comb case bottom, sized for pattern
- Alder, ⅛" (3mm) thick: folding comb case top, sized for pattern
- Ash veneer, layered to ⅛" (3mm) thick: folding comb, sized for pattern
- Wood glue
- Tape: blue painter's
- Spray adhesive
- Sandpaper: assorted grits up to 220
- Pivot pin, ¼" (6mm)-dia.: ½" (1.3cm) long
- Walnut stain
- Turpentine oil
- Beeswax
- Essential oil (optional)

TOOLS

- Scroll saw with blades: #3 reverse-tooth
- CNC machine (optional)
- Chip carving knife
- Drill with bits: assorted small
- #5 gouge: ¼" (6mm)
- #9 gouge: ⅛" (3mm)
- Brush: medium-to-coarse
- Clamps: small

The author used these products for the project. Substitute your choice of brands, tools, and materials as desired.

Butterfly Keepsake Box

Adapt this simple box design to create any number of unique looks

By Tom Noller

As a chip carver, when I look at something made of wood, I immediately imagine how I can embellish it. When I attended a demonstration on making band saw boxes, I realized I can make them of any shape. I enjoy making simple keepsake boxes, like this one, because there is no complex joinery required to build them.

Getting Started

I used a band saw with a ¼" (6mm)-wide, 6-tooth-per-inch (tpi) blade and a scroll saw with a #9 blade. You can make your box almost any width, but the thickness is limited to what you can cut with a scroll saw or coping saw (approximately 2", or 5.1cm). If you use a band saw to cut the center of the box, you'll need to cut a separate lid liner. Just trace the interior of the box sides onto 3/16" (5mm)-thick wood and cut it out.

It's easy to adapt this idea to different chip-carving patterns—just trace a box shape around the chip design and cut it as shown here. We've added some bonus patterns on pages 11 and 12. If the box is unstable on its side, temporarily attach it to a square board when you slice off the top and bottom for safety.

MAKING THE BOX

1 **Attach the pattern to the blank.** Cut the perimeter with a band saw. Rip a ⅛" (3mm)-thick slice from the bottom. Rip a ¼" (6mm)-thick slice off the top. Mark the top and bottom of the center section.

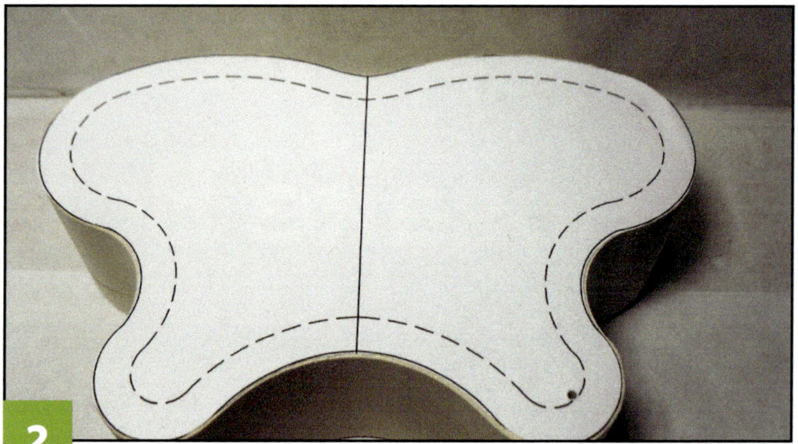

2 **Attach the body pattern to the top of the center section.** Drill a blade-entry hole just inside the inner line. Insert a scroll saw or coping saw blade and cut the center. Go slowly and let the blade do the work. *Note: This wood is thick and will take time to cut.* Mark the top and bottom of the box sides and the cutout.

3 **Rip a 3⁄16" (5mm) slice from the top of the center cutout.** Use the band saw. This will be the lid liner. Depending on the size of your box, you might be able to use what remains of this center section to make another box.

4 **Glue the slice you cut in Step 3 to the inside of the top.** Use the body of the box to center it in place. You need to have a slight space all around the insert so the top will sit comfortably without getting stuck. Carefully remove the body and clamp the insert to the top without moving it. Don't use too much glue or it will tend to slide. Wipe away any squeeze-out so it will not interfere with the top fitting.

5 **Sand the inside of the box sides and the top of the bottom.** Then, glue and clamp the bottom to the sides. Remove any squeeze-out from the inside of the body. Check the fit of the top, and sand the top and bottom with 220-grit sandpaper.

CARVING THE DESIGN

6 **Transfer the chip-carving pattern to the top.** Carve the chips. Then, finish the box. I use Minwax golden pecan stain. When the stain is dry, apply a clear spray finish. Add flocking to the inside of the box if desired.

Butterfly Box Patterns

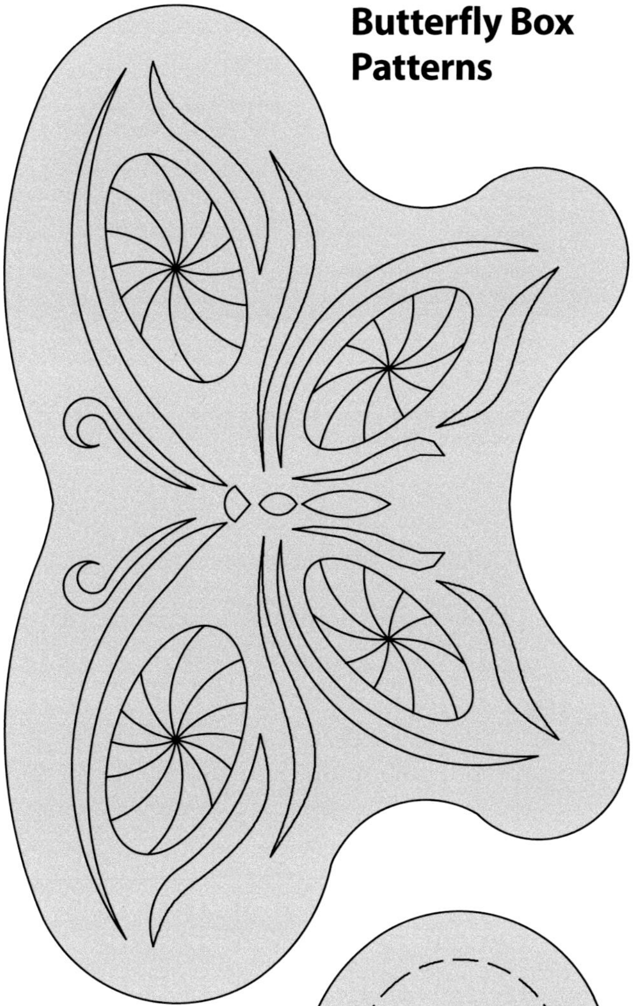

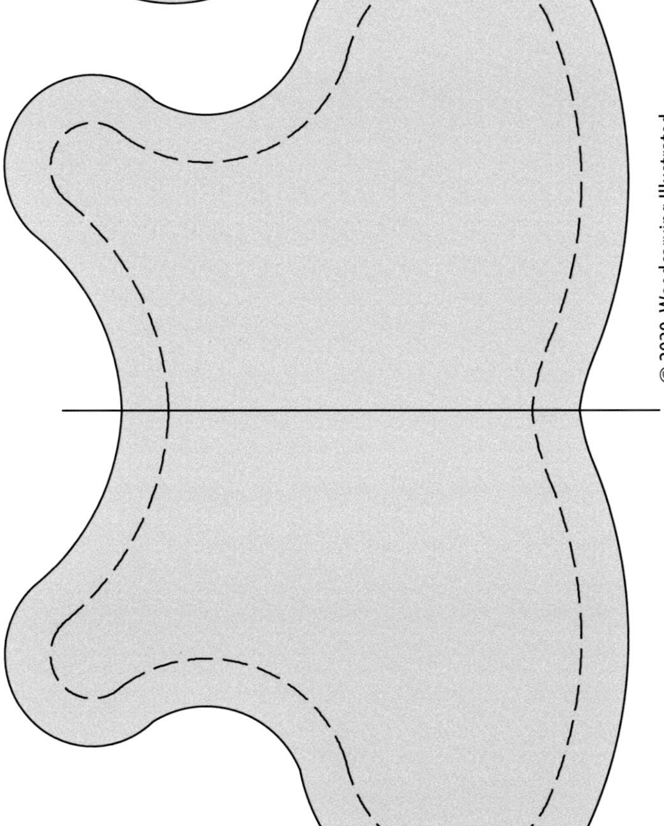

Alternate Chip Carved Box Patterns

Pattern from *Chip Carving - The Best of Woodcarving Illustrated*

Pattern from *Chip-Carved Christmas Ornaments*

Pattern from *Chip-Carved Christmas Ornaments*

materials & **tools**

MATERIALS

- Basswood, 2" (5.1cm) thick: 3½" x 5½" (8.9cm x 14cm)
- Sandpaper: 220 grit
- Wood glue
- Stain, such as Minwax golden pecan
- Finish: clear spray
- Flocking (optional)

TOOLS

- Band saw with blade: ¼" (6mm) wide (6tpi)
- Scroll saw with blades: #9 reverse-tooth
- Chip carving knife
- Clamps: small

The author used these products for the project. Substitute your choice of brands, tools, and materials as desired.

Alternate Chip Carved Box Patterns

Pattern from *Chip-Carved Christmas Ornaments*

Pattern from *Chip Carving - The Best of Woodcarving Illustrated*

Trio of Barrettes

Use old-world or Swiss-style chip carving to beautify barrettes

By Steve Reed

A couple of years ago, I was looking for a Valentine's Day gift for my lovely wife and found some barrette blanks at a carving show. She has long hair, and I thought they would be perfect. I chip carved a barrette for her and she was thrilled. Her friends loved them, too; since then, I've made about 50 barrettes for gifts and local craft shows.

Preparing the Blank

Begin by sanding the barrette blank with a 400-grit sanding block to freshen the surface and make it very smooth.

I draw the pattern directly onto the wood rather than carving through paper or using a transfer tool. Use a 0.5mm mechanical pencil and make light lines so you don't dent the blank with the lead. Using a flexible ruler, find the center of the barrette horizontally and vertically to determine the center point of the piece. Draw a horizontal line through the center to the length of the pattern. You can use a compass to create a rosette in the center or multiple rosettes along the length. For triangular or other geometric chips, I find it simpler to measure in millimeters instead of fractions. A drafting square, such as Rotring's Centro Geo Set Square, makes it easy to determine the center point between two lines.

Carving Old-World-Style Chips

Old-world-style chips are usually triangular, with the deepest part of the chip at the tip of the triangle. With practice, you can carve another, smaller, old-world chip inside a larger one.

TIP

PRACTICE ON SCRAP

Before carving a barrette, transfer the pattern to a piece of scrap wood to practice carving. That way, if you make an error, it's on scrap instead of the barrette.

1 **Make the first cut.** Position the knife perpendicular to the surface of the wood along one of the lines with the tip of the knife on the point of the triangle. Rotate your wrist so the knife cuts into the wood. The knife cuts deepest at the point and gets shallower as you approach the base of the triangle.

2 **Make the second cut.** Position the knife perpendicular to the surface of the wood along the other line and repeat the process.

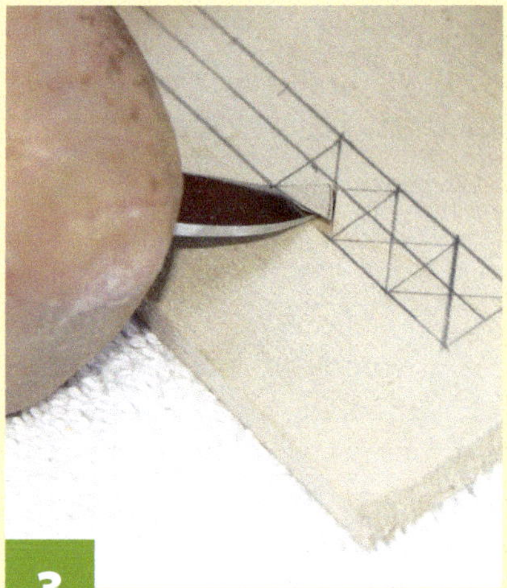

3 **Free the chip.** Hold the knife at a shallow angle with its tip on one side of the base line. Slice in with the knife at a shallow angle until the tip reaches the point of the triangle (the deepest part). Rotate your wrist as needed to cut the rest of the way along the base line and free the chip.

Embellishing with a Stab Knife

I make most of the cuts with a standard chip carving knife. However, in the center of the diamonds on the old-world-style barrette, I used a stab knife to carve simple crosses. Simply press the stab knife in to carve each of the four cuts branching out from the center.

Carving Swiss-Style Chips

For Swiss-style chips (rosettes, organic forms, and geometric chips), the deepest part of the chip is usually in the center. No matter how many sides the chips have, hold the knife at the same angle as you cut the sides of the chip so the cuts meet in the center. For rosettes, make the deepest cuts first, removing the area between the petals. Once you remove the wood around all four petals, carve the small triangles at the ends of the petals.

To keep from breaking a nearby chip, always start a new chip with the knife blade angled away from the just-carved chip. To keep from carving yourself into a corner, start at one end of the line and work your way to the other end. That way, you won't need to carve a chip centered between two already-carved chips.

Finishing the Barrette

Erase any pattern lines with a white polymer eraser. Don't rub too hard, as you can damage the delicate points of the design. Lightly sand the project with the 400-grit sanding block to remove any extra marks or finger smudges. Spray the barrette with at least two coats of semigloss finish. Use a maroon Scotch-Brite™ pad to smooth the piece, and then remove any dust with a tack cloth. Spray on another coat or two of semigloss finish. To make the chips stand out, apply a dark gel stain and immediately wipe it off. The stain will settle into the chips to make them slightly darker than the surface. Be careful—if the project isn't sealed well, the stain can bleed.

If you prefer, before carving the barrette, paint it with full-strength acrylic or craft paint, and then carve the design through the paint. This works especially well with holiday designs (painted red or green) or designs inspired by Asian lacquerware (painted black).

Barrette Patterns

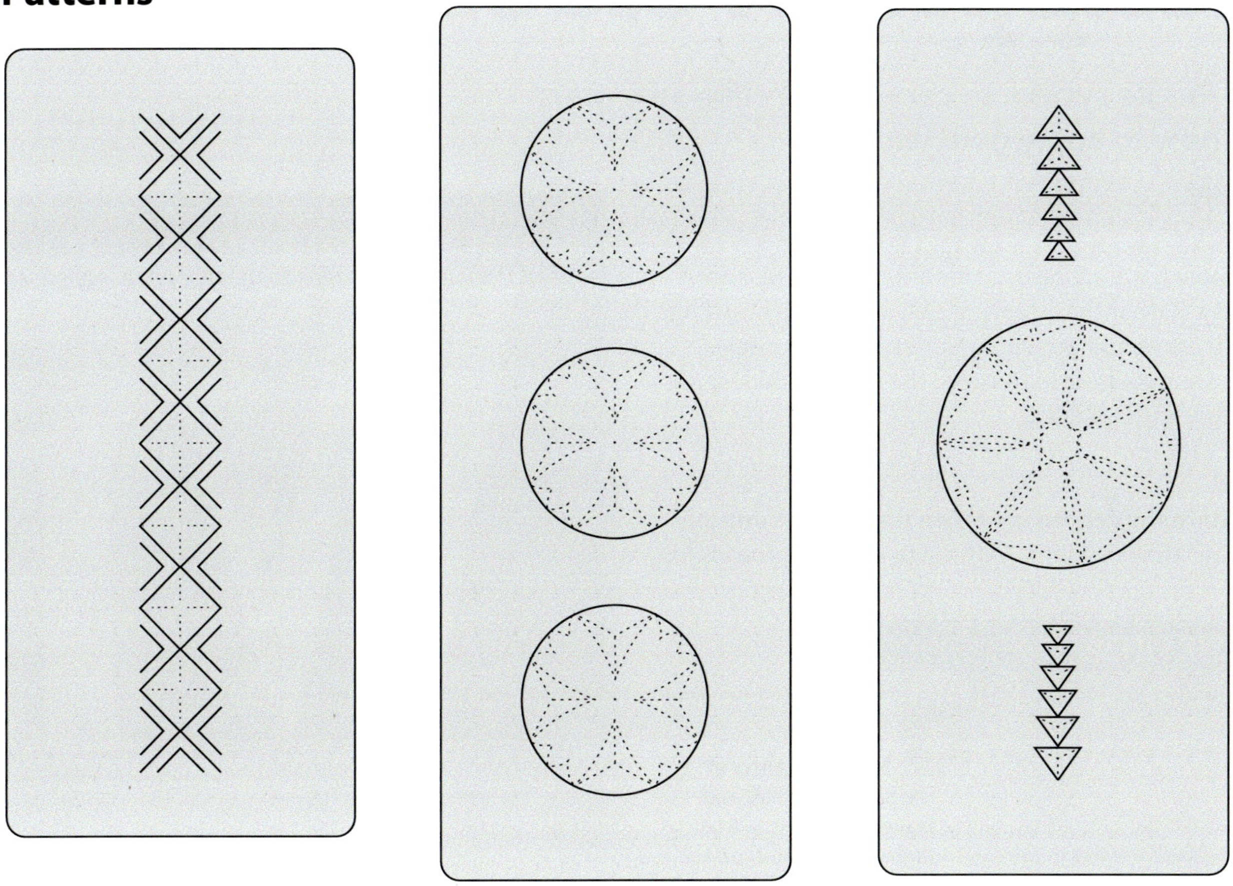

materials & **tools**

MATERIALS

- Barrette blank: 1⅞" x 4" (4.8cm x 10.2cm) or 1⅞" x 4½" (4.8cm x 11.4cm)
- Sanding block: 400-grit
- Sanding pad, such as Scotch-Brite™: maroon
- Finish: semigloss
- Gel stain: dark
- Tack cloth
- Acrylic paints: assorted
- Mechanical pencil: 0.5mm

TOOLS

- Knives: chip carving, stab
- Drafting square, such as Rotring's Centro Geo Set Square (optional)
- Flexible ruler
- Eraser: white polymer

The author used these products for the project. Substitute your choice of brands, tools, and materials as desired.

Pineapple Welcome Sign

Follow this simple system to carve letters like an expert
Plus! Learn how to apply gold leaf

By Vernon DePauw

The pineapple has long been a symbol of welcome and hospitality. Rather than carving down the entire surface of the sign, we'll carve and attach the pineapple separately. Then we'll use a simple system to carve the letters and learn how to add a glow with gold leaf.

Getting Started

Enlarge the patterns as desired, and then transfer the outlines to the blanks. Cut the perimeter of the sign and the pineapple.

CARVING THE PINEAPPLE

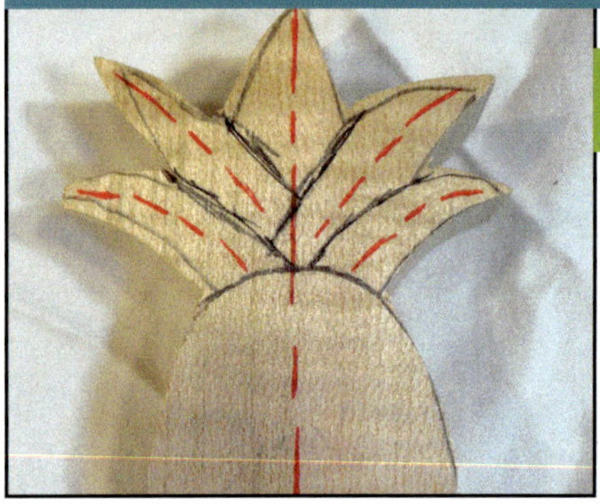

1 **Mark the center of the pineapple fruit and leaves.** These lines will be the highest (thickest) part of the fruit and each leaf.

2 **Carve the leaves.** Use a carving knife. Leave the centers thick, and carve a groove between the leaves.

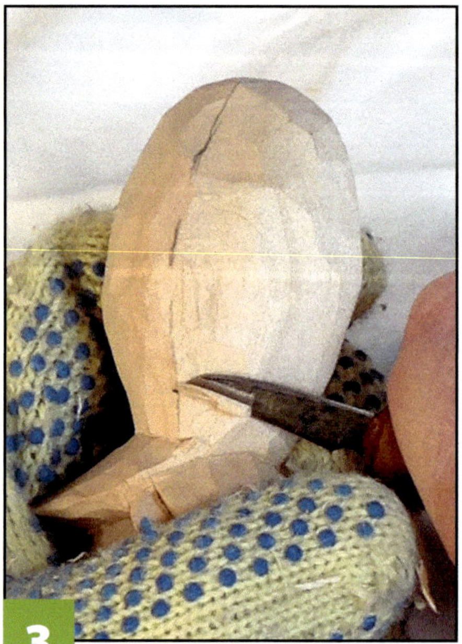

3 **Round the fruit from the centerline to the edges.** Use the knife.

4 **Back-cut the back edge of the pineapple the entire way around.** Add the details to the fruit and leaves.

CARVING THE LETTERS

5 **Transfer the letter pattern to the sign.** Use carbon paper. I use Times New Roman font, which is a serif font. Serifs are the decorative elements added to the basic form of each letter, and I like the look of serif fonts for carving.

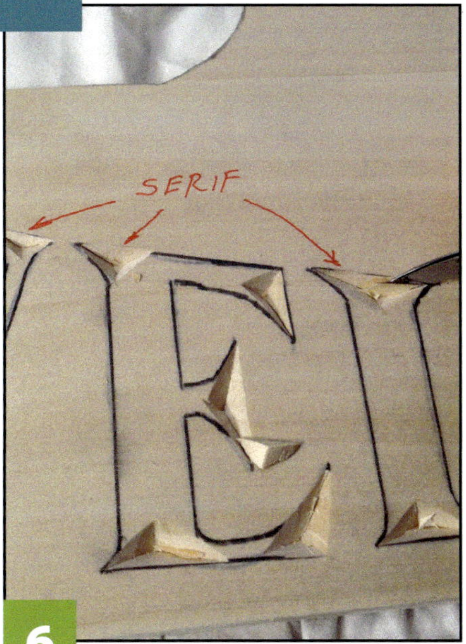

6 **Carve the serifs.** Use the knife to make a three-sided chip-style cut for each of the serifs.

7 **Make angled cuts along the inside and outside of each letter.** Use the carving knife. Make the cuts meet in the center to create a V-shaped groove. Refine the edges of the letters. Use the knife. Create crisp edges to give the letters depth and sharpness.

FINISHING THE PROJECT

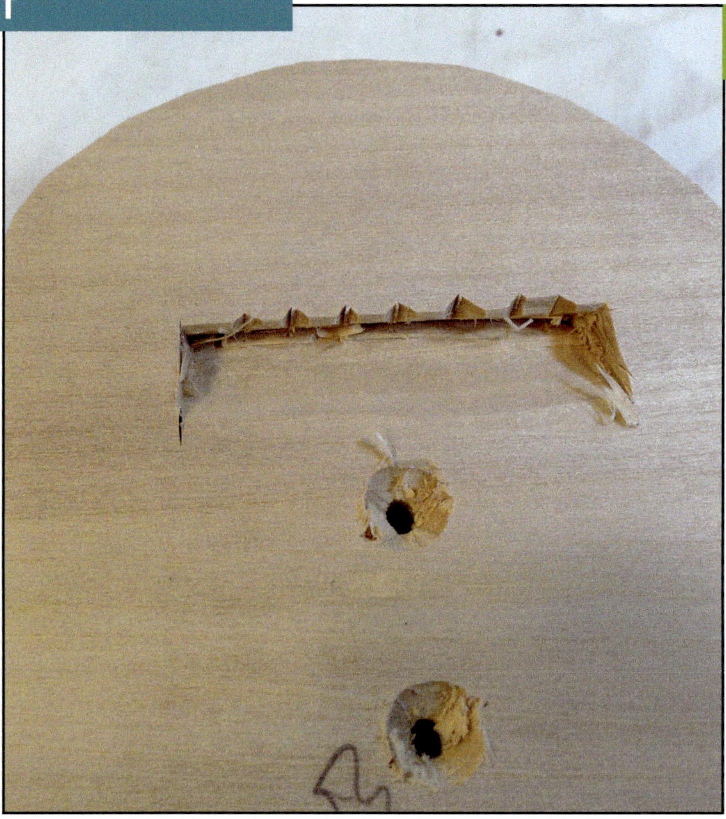

8 **Carve the outside edge of the sign.** You could also soften the edges with 220-grit sandpaper. Position the pineapple and trace around it. Drill two 5⁄32" (4mm)-dia. holes through the sign inside the outline and countersink these holes from the back for the screws used to attach the pineapple to the sign.

9 **Carve a hanging slot in the center of the sign back.** Sand the top surface of the sign to remove any reference lines and prepare it for painting. Apply a little wood glue to the back of the pineapple and hold it in position while driving a screw in from the back. Rotate the pineapple so it is straight up and down, and secure it with the second screw.

PAINTING THE SIGN

10 **Apply two light coats of light gray exterior house primer on all sides of the sign.** I use a light gray because it is easier to cover with a topcoat than white. Use a 1" (25mm)-wide artist brush to spread the paint evenly into the grooves and letters you have carved. Make sure the light coats do not fill in the carved details.

11 **Paint the letters with two coats of white.** Use a ¼" (6mm)-wide angled shader. Do the letters first because you can paint up to the edge of them when painting the top surface to produce a crisp edge. Paint the pineapple fruit goldenrod yellow and the leaves hemlock green, or, if you plan to gild it with gold leaf (see Applying Gold Leaf, page 19), apply two coats of settlers blue to the pineapple and the sign surface front and back. Apply two coats of Helmsman clear satin spar urethane, front and back.

TIP

PICKING PAINT COLORS

When picking your sign colors, keep in mind that you want to create a contrast between the sign, the pineapple, and the letters. To give my sign a Colonial look, I chose to use Olde Century Colors simulated milk paint, which comes in traditional colors and leaves a subtle brush strokes in the finish, like paint from the 1800s.

Applying Gold Leaf

Choosing Materials

The best gold leaf to use for a carving project is 23-karat genuine gold leaf in loose leaf form. It comes in "books," usually of 25 gold sheets, but some suppliers sell five or 10-leaf booklets. For one pineapple, five leaves of gold should be more than enough. Avoid imitation gold, which lacks the luster of real gold and is difficult to apply to a wood carving.

The glue used to attach gold leaf to the carving is called "gilding size." It comes in two drying speeds: slow set and quick set. I prefer slow set because it has a longer open time, which gives you plenty of time to apply the gold. I use soft ½" (13mm)- and 1" (25mm)-wide soft bristle craft brushes to apply the gold leaf and move it into the grooves and crevices.

Getting Started With Gold Leaf

Gold leaf will stick to any surface with even the slightest stickiness to it. To reduce the amount of gold that may stick where you do not want it, first let the sign dry for a few weeks. Use a damp cloth to wipe down the entire sign to remove any remaining stickiness. Then, wipe it dry and let it air-dry overnight. Lightly sprinkle a layer of baby powder over the sign, blowing off any extra. Prepare your work area by turning off any fans or vents, because air movement will affect the even drying of the sizing as well as the application of the gold.

Applying the Leaf

A. Apply the sizing evenly. Use a ½" (13mm)-wide angled shader brush. Apply an even coat to the surfaces and crevices you want gold to stick to, but do not allow it to puddle or run. Thick areas of sizing will dry at a different rate than thin areas.

B. Check the tack of the sized surface. The sizing will dry at different rates based on the humidity and the thickness of the application. Gilding on wet sizing will use a lot of gold and dull the luster. To avoid those problems, let the size dry for 6 to 8 hours, and then check the tack. I use the hairs on the back of my finger. Turn your hand over and slowly lower it to just above the surface until the sizing tugs on the hairs between your knuckles. A gentle tug, like when a mosquito brushes your hair, indicates the size is ready. A tug strong enough to actually pull your hair indicates the size is too wet. As a second test, place a small piece of gold on the sized area, and then see if another small piece will stick to the gold you just placed. If the second piece sticks, the sizing is too wet. Wet sizing will pass through the thin gold leaf and allow the next piece to stick on top. Check the size often until the tack is ready.

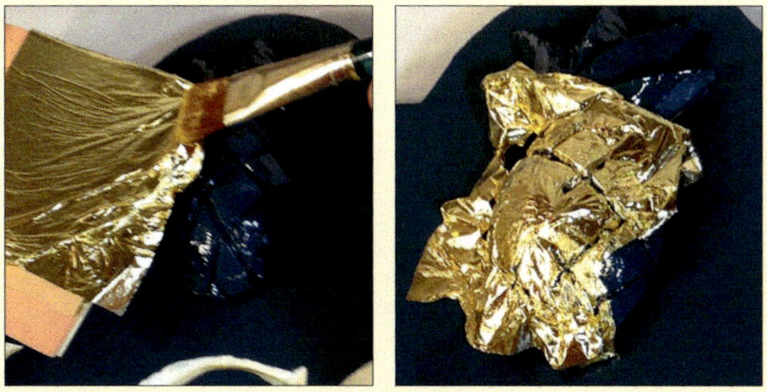

C. Fold back one page of the gold leaf book to expose the gold. Swish the 1" (25mm)-wide brush through your hair to add a little static and oil to the brush. Lower the brush to the leaf; the static will cause a small piece to lift to the brush. Move the gold slowly to the pineapple surface and gently lower it until it sticks to the surface. Continue transferring gold from the book to the carving until the pineapple is covered.

D. Gently brush the pineapple to set the gold in place. Use the 1" (25mm)-wide brush. This should make most of the gold stick to the surface, although some small pieces will flake off. Brush the small pieces into the grooves, adding more gold from the book as needed to cover all of the surfaces and grooves. Brush over the entire pineapple to dislodge any loose gold. If gold will not stick in an area, brush a thin coat of sizing on it, let the sizing set to the proper tack, and reapply the gold.

E. Wipe the gilded area with a clean, damp sponge. This gives it a clean, finished look. Don't add a topcoat over the gold; it may dull the fine luster. If a piece of gold sticks in the wrong place, gently scrape it off with the back of a carving knife.

materials & **tools**

MATERIALS

- Basswood, ¾" (1.9cm) thick: sign, 8" x 20" (20.3cm x 50.8cm); pineapple, 3" x 4" (7.6cm x 10.2cm)
- Carbon paper
- Pencil
- Drywall screws, #8: 2 each 1⅝" (4.1cm) long
- Latex house primer: light gray
- Latex house paint: white
- Milk paint, such as Olde Century: settlers blue, hemlock green (optional), goldenrod yellow (optional)
- Baby powder
- Gold leaf, 23-karat loose: at least 5 leaves
- Gilding size, slow set, such as Rolco clear oil
- Wood glue
- Spar urethane, such as Helmsman: clear satin
- Sandpaper: 220-grit

TOOLS

- Band saw
- Drill with bit: 5⁄32" (4mm)-dia.
- Chip carving knife
- Screwdriver
- Paintbrushes: ¼" (6mm)-wide angled shader, ½" (13mm)-wide angled shader, 1" (25mm)-wide artist, ½" (13mm)-wide soft craft, 1" (25mm)-wide soft craft
- Small sponge

The author used these products for the project. Substitute your choice of brands, tools, and materials as desired.

Welcome Sign Pattern

Each block of this grid equals 1" in proportion to the original pattern. Enlarge this art to 200%, or to desired size.

Perpetual Calendar

Customize this project with chip- and relief-carved embellishments

Original design by Paul Meisel
Text and carved version by Andrew DiPace

Perpetual calendars have been around for many years. I liked the idea of changing the calendar each month to suit my needs, so I purchased plans around 15 years ago from Meisel Hardware Specialties. It took me awhile, but I finally made one.

Because I'm a carver, I chip-carved the placards for the numbers, months, and days. The plans come with patterns for nine seasonal embellishments, including a heart, flag, and Christmas tree. I found free clip art online and designed a few more, such as a cross for Easter. I also carved designs on extra date tiles for holidays and events like birthdays and appointments.

Making the Project

To make this version, pictured at left, cut the pieces to the sizes noted in the parts list. I suggest that you rip several basswood strips for the month and numbers at one time, which lets you choose the tiles for the days to avoid hidden knots. (I made a few extra tiles to embellish later as the inspiration strikes me.) Sand the pieces smooth using 220-grit sandpaper and refer to the assembly guide as you glue and clamp the pieces together.

My calendar is slightly different. I adapted the pattern by stretching it taller to add extra rails, and then I changed the month and day-of-the-week markers into sliding tiles. I installed removable side framing so the tiles can't fall out and added a drawer and a top-open compartment. I tweaked the roof and eliminated the bird so it looks less like a birdhouse.

The original project attaches the interchangeable embellishments via a hole and dowel system. Instead, I glued a strong magnet into a recess drilled in the base and then glued a steel washer into a recess drilled in the back of each carving.

Paul Meisel's original perpetual calendar.

Carving the Pieces

I cut the embellishments on a scroll saw, and then used a knife and a selection of gouges to round the edges and carve the details. For the month, day, and date tiles, I chose an alphabet and numbers and carved them free-form. I also added designs to the drawer front and sides. I sourced the drawer embellishment designs from Lora S. Irish's *Chip Carving Workshop*. I sketched clip-art-style designs for appointments, holidays, birthdays, etc. on extra tiles and then carved and woodburned them as necessary.

Finishing the Project

Seal the basswood pieces with a mixture of equal parts boiled linseed oil and mineral spirits (brushed on or dipped). After that mixture dries, paint as desired and seal with a satin varnish, such as JoSonja water-based polyurethane. Finish the rest of the pieces with semigloss polyurethane, such as Minwax.

Andy sketched and relief-carved nine seasonal embellishments. **See the heart on page 21.**

FURTHER READING

Chip Carving Workshop
by Lora S. Irish

Item 7766. Available for $16.99 + S&H (parcel post) from Fox Chapel Publishing, 800-457-9112, FoxChapelPublishing.com, or your local retailer.

Perpetual Calendar Patterns

Perpetual Calendar Assembly Drawing

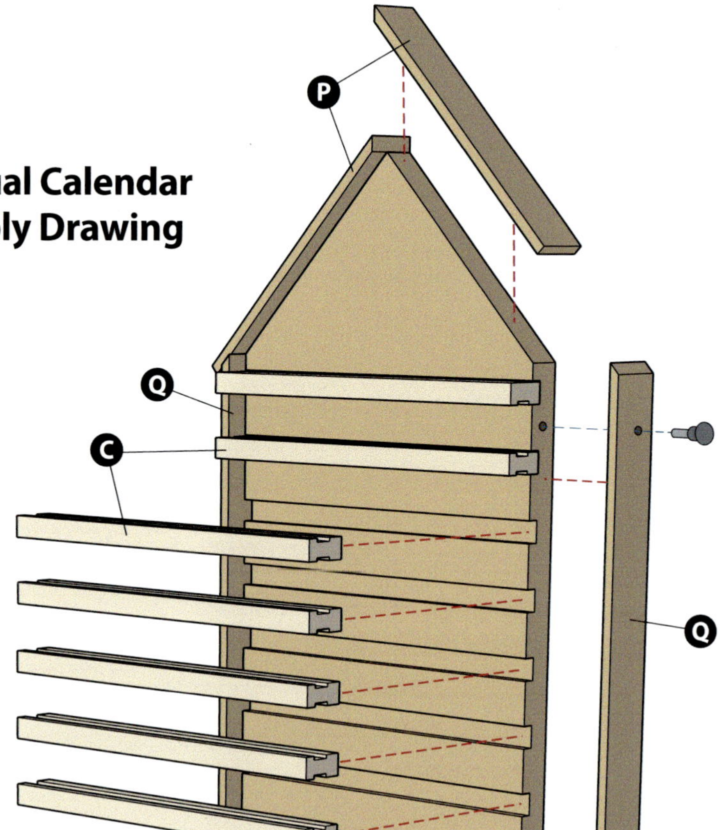
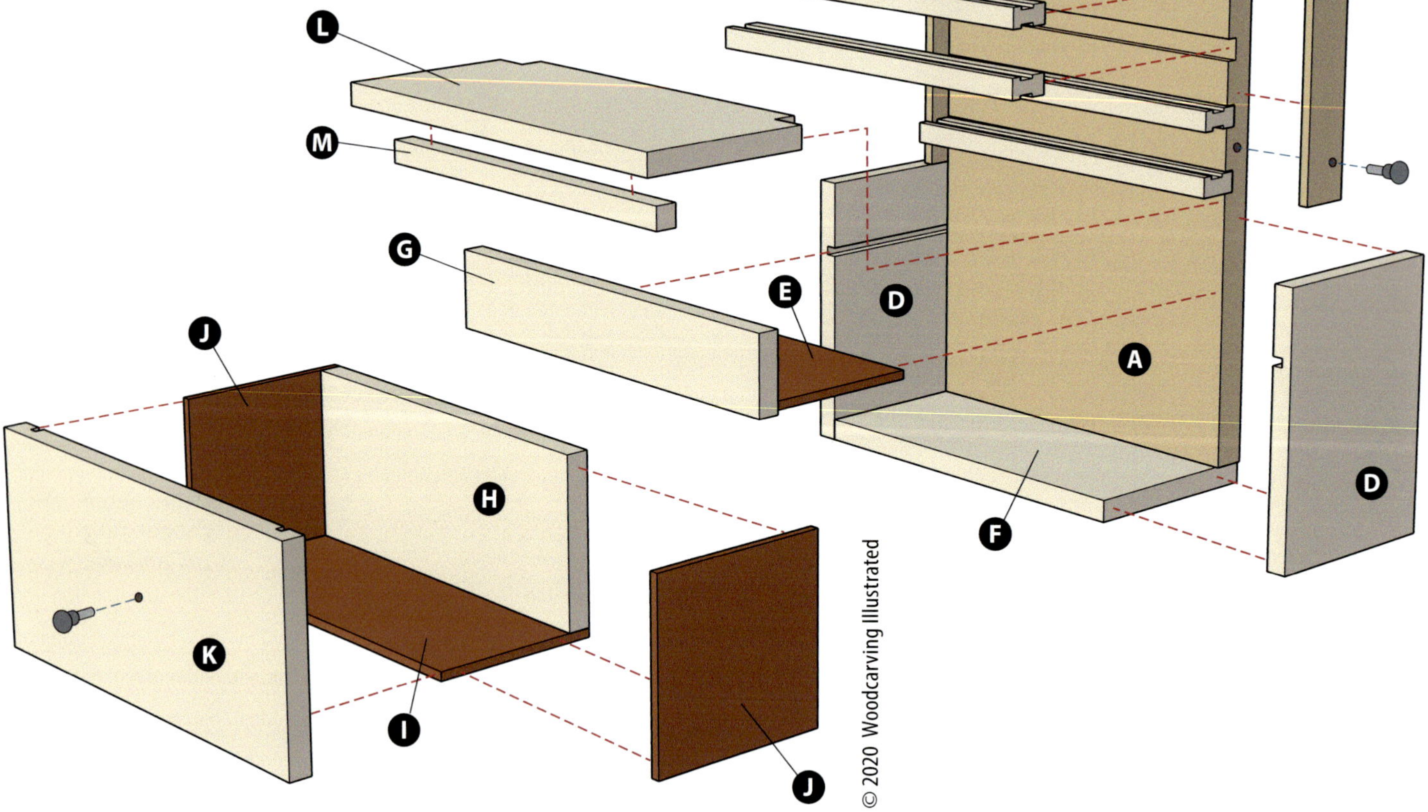

Parts List

	Item	Quantity	Materials	Dimensions	Notes
A	Back/Base	1	Oak veneer plywood, ¾" (1.9cm) thick	9" x 25¼" (22.9cm x 64.1cm)	Cut top at a 45° angle for peak.
B	Embellishments	1	Basswood, 1" (2.5cm) thick	12" x 14" (30.5cm x 35.6cm)	
C	Rails	9	Basswood, ½" (1.3cm) thick	1" x 9" (2.5cm x 22.9cm)	
D	Storage compartment sides	2	Basswood, ½" (1.3cm) thick	4½" x 6¼" (11.4cm x 15.9cm)	
E	Storage compartment divider	1	Lauan mahogany plywood, 3⁄16" (5mm) thick	3 13⁄16" x 9 5⁄16" (9.7cm x 23.7cm)	
F	Storage compartment bottom	1	Basswood, ½" (1.3cm) thick	4 9⁄16" x 8 15⁄16" (11.6cm x 22.7cm)	
G	Storage compartment front	1	Basswood, ½" (1.3cm) thick	1¾" x 9 15⁄16" (4.4cm x 25.3cm)	
H	Storage drawer back	1	Basswood, ½" (1.3cm) thick	3 9⁄16" x 8½" (9.1cm x 21.6cm)	
I	Storage drawer bottom	1	Lauan mahogany plywood, 3⁄16" (5mm) thick	3 13⁄16" x 8½" (9.7cm x 21.6cm)	
J	Storage drawer sides	2	Lauan mahogany plywood, 3⁄16" (5mm) thick	3¾" x 3 13⁄16" (9.5cm x 9.7cm)	
K	Storage drawer front	1	Basswood, ½" (1.3cm) thick	4½" x 9 15⁄16 (11.4cm x 25.3cm)	
L	Storage box top	1	Basswood, ½" (1.3cm) thick	4 9⁄16" x 9 15⁄16" (11.6cm x 25.3cm)	Do not glue – panel lifts free. Notch back corners to fit.
M	Storage box top cleat	1	Basswood, ⅜" (1cm) thick	½" x 8⅞" (1.3cm x 22.5cm)	
N	Day of the week blocks	7	Basswood, ⅜" (1cm) thick	1¼" (3.2cm) square	
O	Month strips	12	Basswood, ⅜" (1cm) thick	1¼" x 8⅞" (3.2cm x 22.5cm)	
P	Roof	2	Oak, ¼" (6mm) thick	1½" x 7 7⁄16" (3.8cm x 18.9cm)	Cut top ends at 45° angle
Q	Sides	2	Oak, ¼" (6mm) thick	1½" x 15" (3.8cm x 38.1cm)	Cut top ends at 45° angle
R	Number blanks	At least 42	Basswood, ⅜" (1cm) thick	1¼" (3.2cm) square	Dimensions

materials & **tools**

MATERIALS:

- Oak veneer plywood, ¾" (1.9cm) thick: 9" x 25¼" (22.9cm x 64.1cm)
- Basswood, 1" (2.5cm) thick: 12" x 14" (30.5cm x 35.6cm)
- Basswood, ½" (1.3cm) thick: 5" x 70" (12.7cm x 1.8m)
- Basswood, ⅜" (1cm) thick: 6" x 40" (15.2cm x 101.6cm)
- Lauan mahogany plywood, 3⁄16" (5mm) thick: 8" x 13" (20.3cm x 33cm)
- Oak, ¼" (6mm) thick: 5" x 15" (12.7cm x 38.1cm)
- Drawer knobs, brass: ½" (13mm)-dia., 3 each
- Ceramic magnet: ½" (13mm)-dia.
- Steel washer: ⅝" (16mm)-dia. (outside)
- Hangman picture hanging system: 6" (15.2cm)
- Side panel nuts: 2 each #10-32
- Brass flat head wood screws: 6 each #4 x ⅜" (10mm)
- Adhesives: 5-minute epoxy, wood glue
- Polyurethane: semigloss
- Varnish, such as JoSonja: satin
- Boiled linseed oil
- Mineral spirits
- Acrylic paints

TOOLS:

- Table saw
- Router with bits: straight
- Knives: chip carving, stab, bench, detail
- Micro tools, such as Dockyard: 1⁄16" (2mm), ⅛" (3mm), 5⁄32" (4mm), 3⁄16" (5mm)
- V-tool: small 75°
- #3 gouge: 1" (25mm)
- #5 gouge: ⅝" (16mm)
- #7 gouge: ⅝" (16mm)
- #9 gouge: ⅜" (10mm)
- Woodburner with small skew tip

The author used these products for the project. Substitute your choice of brands, tools, and materials as desired.

Perpetual Calendar Measured Drawing

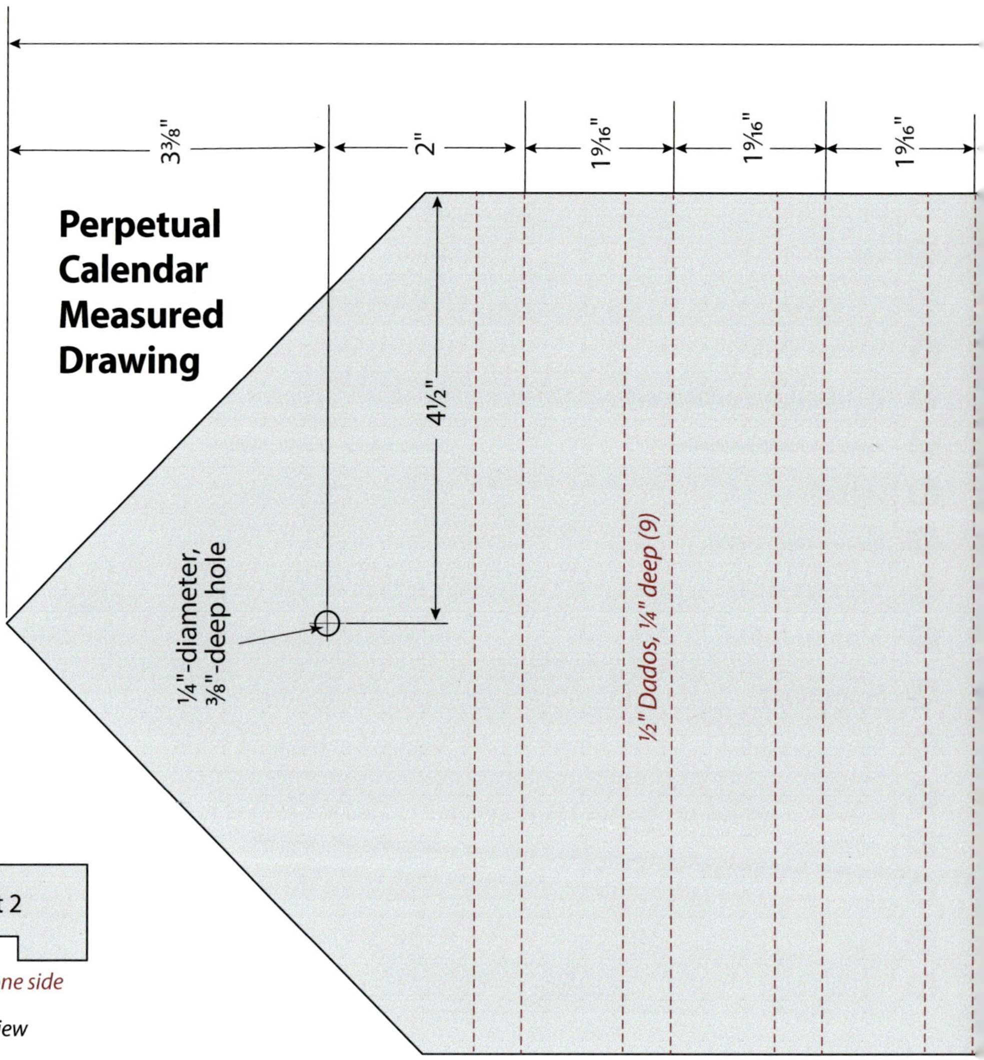

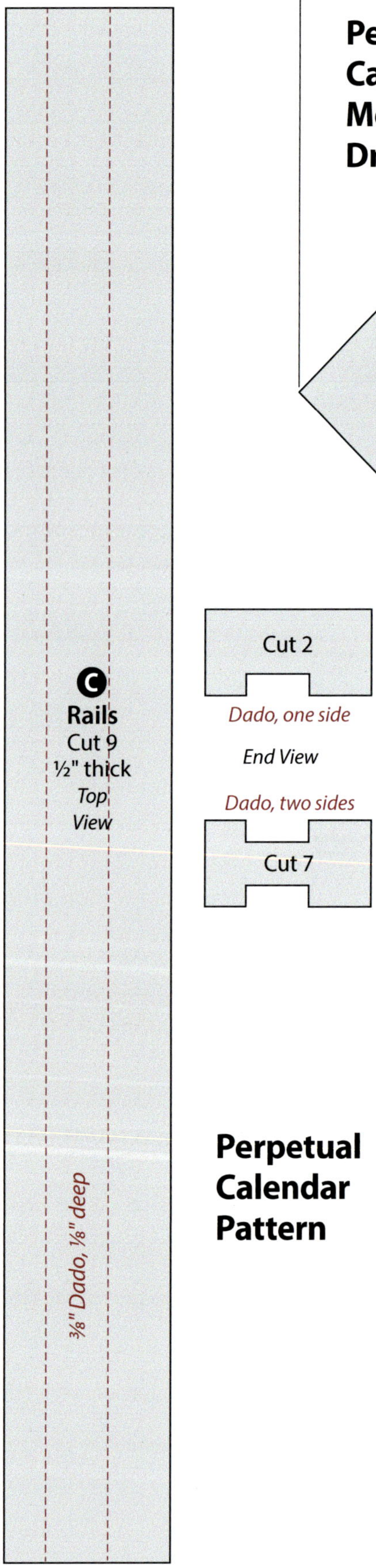

Perpetual Calendar Pattern

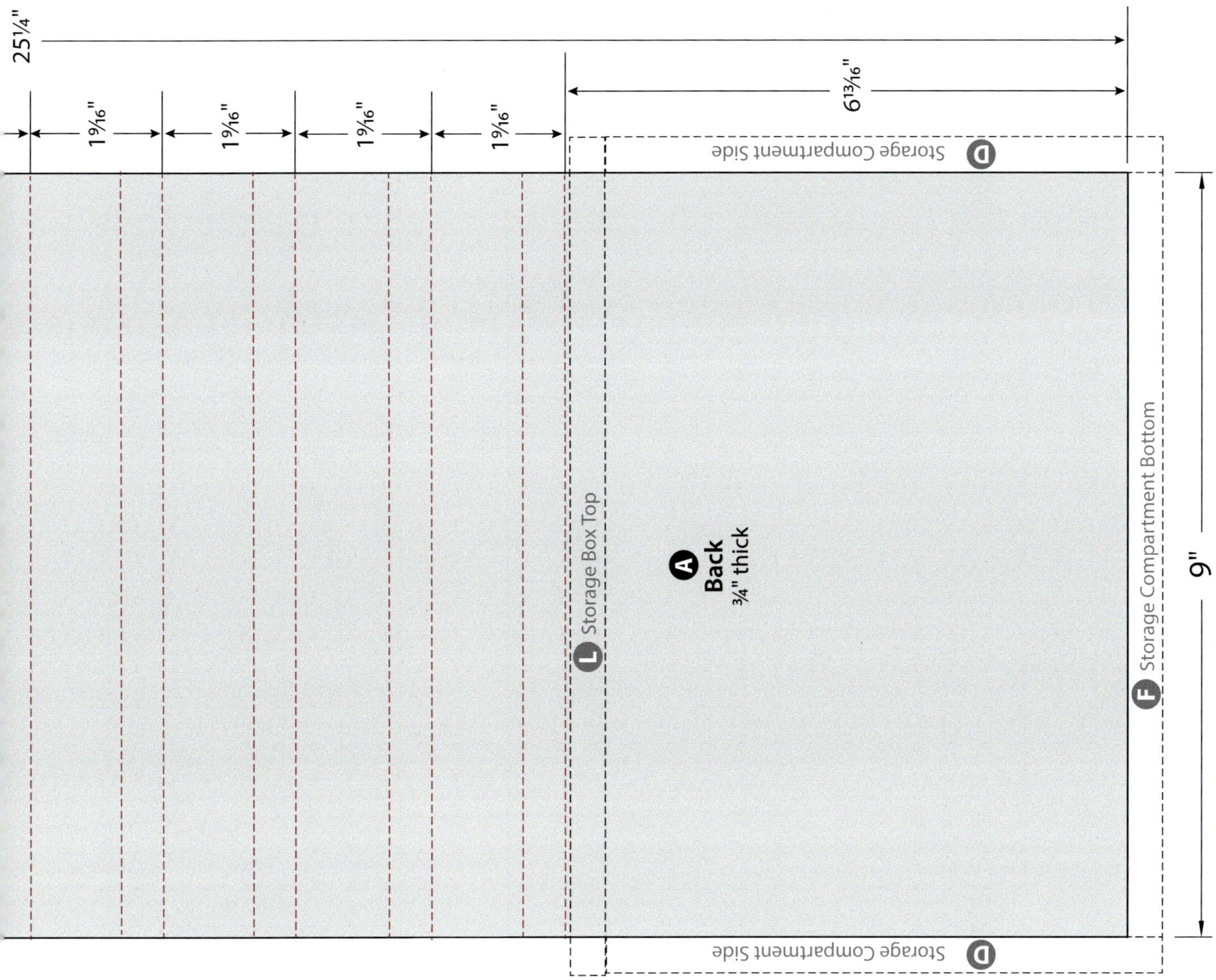

Perpetual Calendar Pattern

Perpetual Calendar Patterns

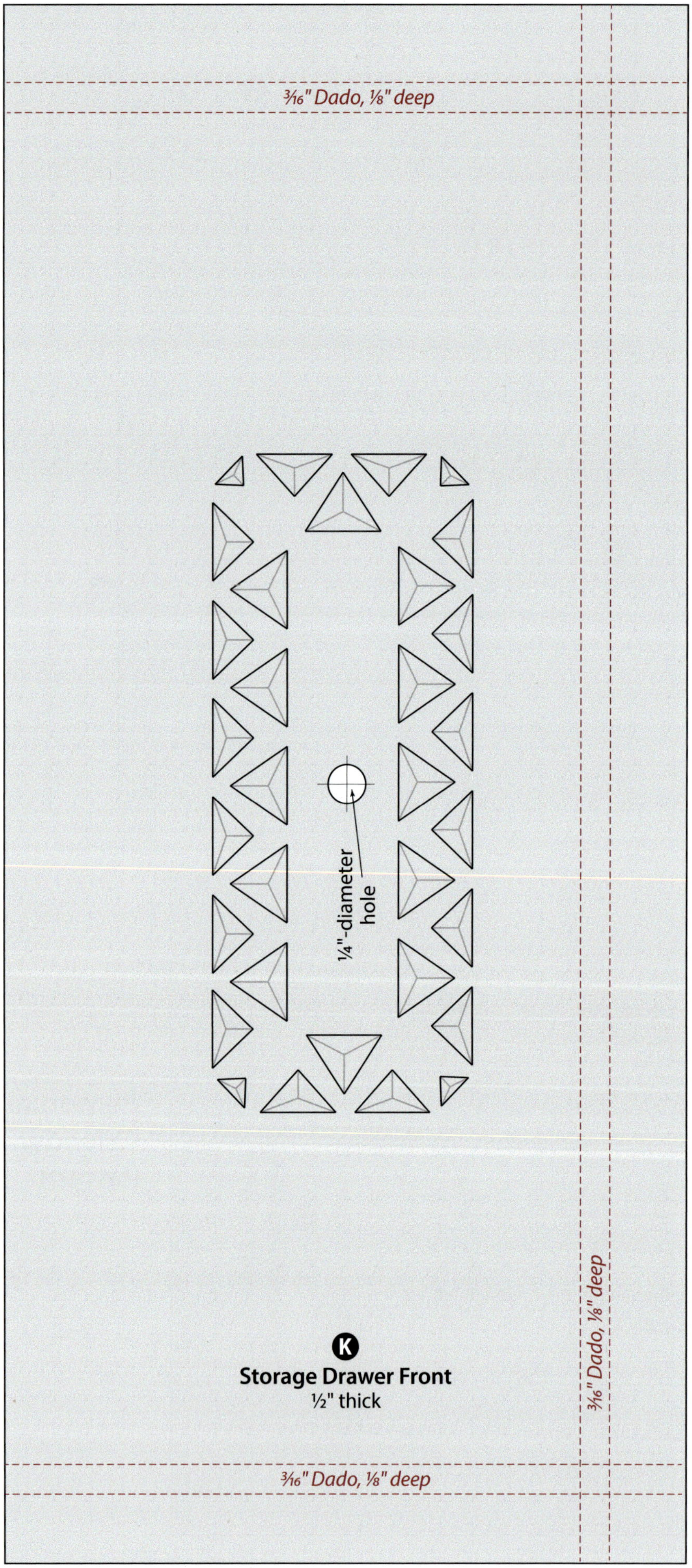

K
Storage Drawer Front
½" thick

G
Storage Compartment Front
½" thick

Rosette Cribbage Board

Learn to carve a classic design by decorating a plate or game board

By Marty Leenhouts

A rosette is a classic design you can use to embellish almost anything, such as a box top, furniture, door, or mantle. Here, we're carving an 8" (20.3cm)-diameter rosette into the center of a cribbage board. (Don't play cribbage? Make a plate or plaque instead.) It's large enough for you to learn the techniques. Then, you can increase or reduce the size of the pattern to fit other items.

If you are uncertain about a portion of the pattern, carve it on a practice board before you try it on your project. Practicing first makes for a much more enjoyable and successful chip carving.

Getting Started

Sand the surface with progressively finer grits of sandpaper up to 220 grit. Transfer the pattern to the blank; I use a Pattern Transfer Tool (see Special Sources on page 28), but you could trace the pattern onto the blank using graphite paper. Cut the perimeter of the blank and drill the peg holes. Or, use a purchased blank.

CARVING THE ROSETTE

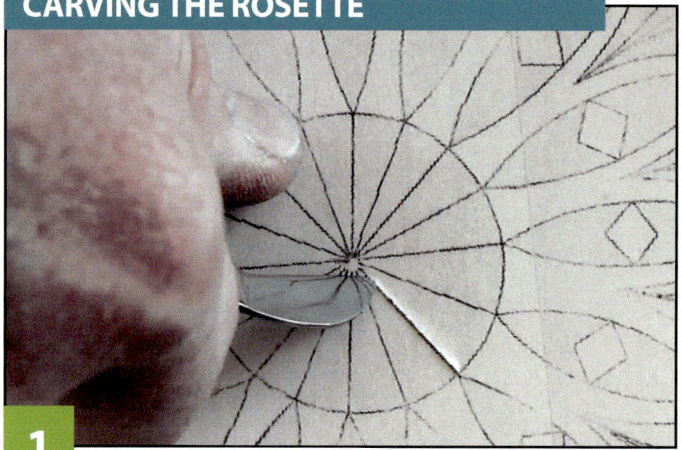

1

Position your hand in the center of the rosette and work out from there. That way you don't have to rest your hand on areas you've already carved. Make the first cut on one of the angled lines parallel with the grain. Work around the center of the pattern in a counterclockwise direction so you will make the last cut, adjacent to the first cut, with the grain. Following this order of cuts will help remove the last chip without any chip-out.

2

Make the four outside cuts around the Gothic leaf shapes. Then, make a cut to remove the majority of one-half of the shape. Then, finish carving this chip by placing the point in the bottom of the chip as you cut. This cut ensures that the ridge and the valley meet in the center and bottom of the chip. Repeat these same cuts on the other side of the leaf.

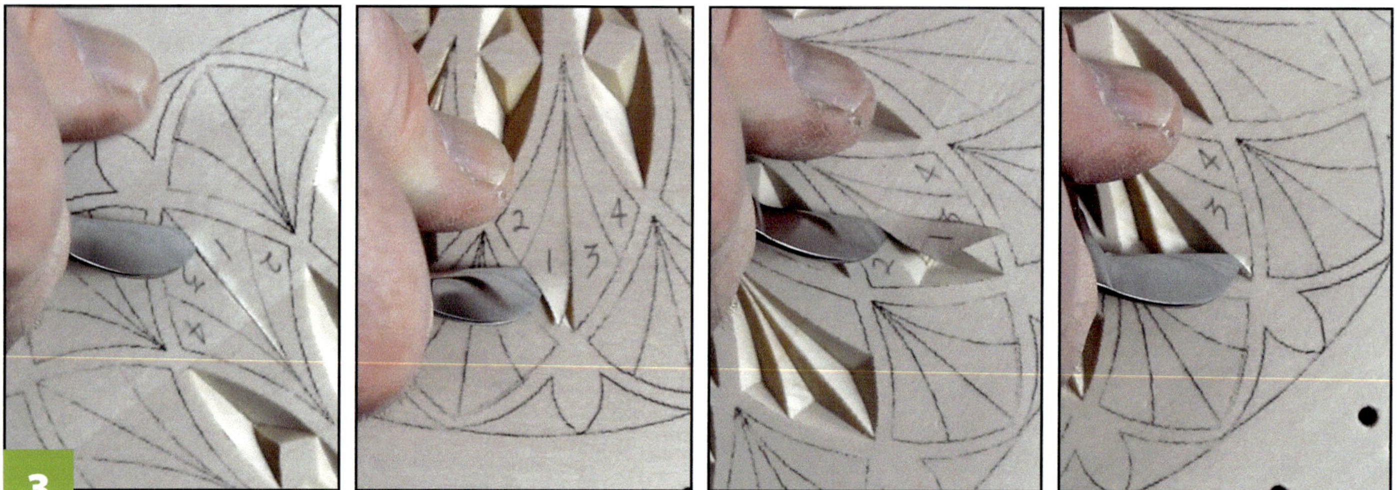

3

Carve the first of four chips in the fan-shaped designs. Each chip requires four cuts. There's not necessarily a right or wrong order of cuts on these fan shapes, but I've found success by starting from the centerline and working out on each side of the fan.

4

Make the inside cuts on all of the three-corner chips on the outer rim. To free the chips, make the final cut along the outside line in one continuous, fluid motion. *Note: If you stop and start often on these cuts, the border will look ragged.*

TIP

PREVENT SPLIT CHIPS

Make the first cut on a new chip with the knife angled away from the adjacent chip you just finished. This will prevent the chips from splitting out.

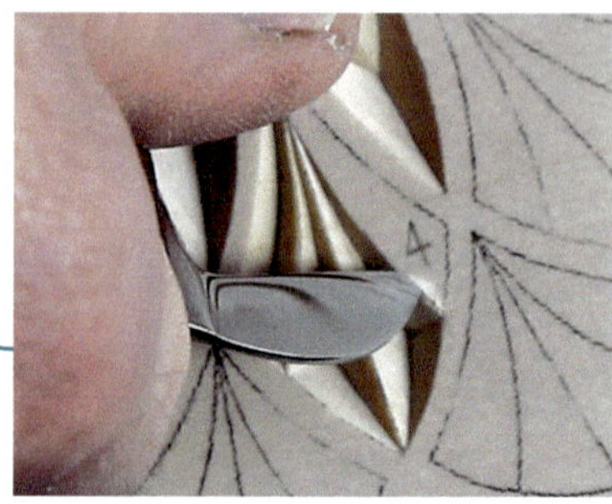

FINISHING THE BOARD

5 **Erase the remaining pattern lines.** Use a Tombow Sand Eraser, and erase carefully, using just enough pressure to remove the black lines. Vacuum off the dust. Apply three or four light coats of clear satin spray acrylic or lacquer to all surfaces.

6 **Brush gel stain into a small area in the center of the carving.** Brush out any extra stain left in the recesses. Wrap a cotton rag tightly around your finger and wipe off the stain on the surface. Wipe the sharp ridges so they stand out. Brush the gel carefully on the outside rim. Avoid getting gel stain outside the rosette. Immediately wipe off any stain that is accidentally brushed outside the border. After the gel stain has dried completely, apply a final coat of clear spray finish.

Drilling Template

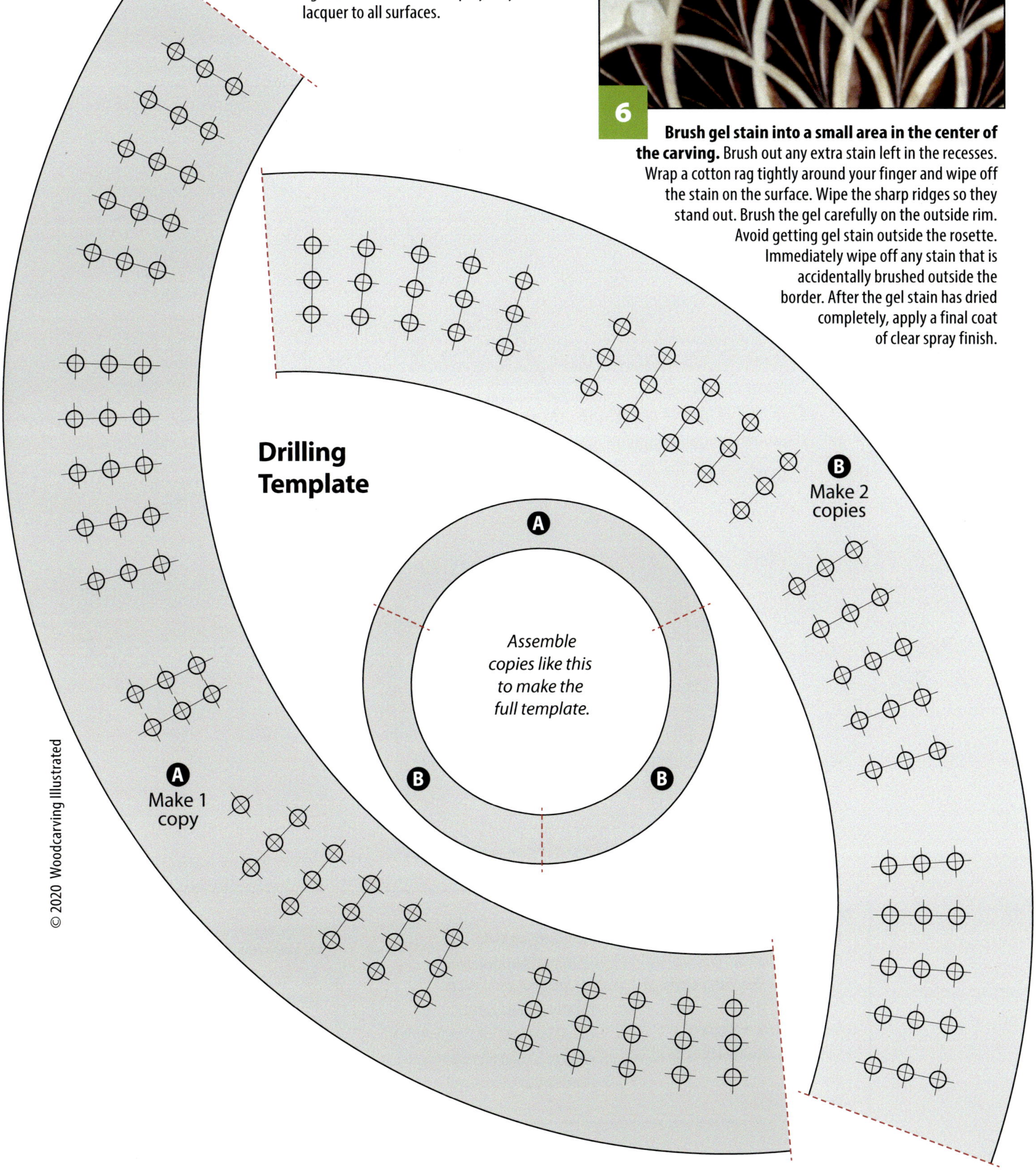

Cribbage Board Rosette Pattern

materials & **tools**

MATERIALS

- Basswood, ¾" (1.9cm) thick: 11½" (29.2cm) square (or precut blank)
- Spray finish: clear satin acrylic or lacquer
- Gel stain: dark mahogany
- Sandpaper: assorted grits up to 220
- Vacuum
- Clean cotton rag

TOOLS

- Chip carving knife
- Pattern Transfer Tool or graphite transfer paper
- Tombow Sand Eraser
- Band saw or scroll saw (optional)
- Drill press and bits (optional)
- Paintbrush

The author used these products for the project. Substitute your choice of brands, tools, and materials as desired.

SPECIAL SOURCES

Basswood cribbage boards, chip-carving knives, Pattern Transfer Tools, and Tombow Sand Erasers are available from MyChipCarving.com.

Simple Cereal Bowl

Embellish turned objects with this clever repeating design

By Amy Costello

As a turner and chip carver, I'm always looking for new ways to combine these skills in interesting ways. After gluing a basswood stripe for carving into a cribbage board I made for my dad, I was inspired to add a similar stripe to a set of cereal bowls. While carving, do your best to cut each facet with a single stroke; lots of practice and a razor-sharp tool are key!

Preparing the Blank

Carving on bowls comes with its own set of challenges. The biggest issue is that most bowls are turned with the grain running horizontally. This makes for stronger bowls, but it also means that at least half of the carving surface is end grain or similar. End grain is a pain to carve, and I was never quite satisfied with the results I got from simply gluing a rectangle of basswood onto a regular bowl blank. Luckily, the turning world already had an elegant solution that allowed me to create a continuous edge grain surface around the entire bowl. It's called segmenting—gluing several smaller pieces together to form a larger blank.

Make your blank. With segmenting, you can control the orientation of each piece, allowing you to create blanks with ideal grain configuration that would otherwise be impossible to achieve. For my bowls, I made basswood hexagons (basically picture frames with 30° miters instead of 45°) using a miter saw. (Find a template of the hexagon glueup on page 30) Then I resawed a thick chunk of walnut on the band saw, jointed the inside faces, and sandwiched the basswood hexagon between them, clamping the blank tightly. It's important that the glue joint between every piece of the blank is extremely tight; otherwise, you'll end up with hairline holes in your bowl! Let the glue dry and remove the clamps.

Scale up the blank to make larger serving bowls, if desired.

materials & **tools**

MATERIALS

All wood dimensions refer to the size of the blank, not the finished bowl

- Walnut or cherry, 2½" (6.4cm) thick: 6½" (16.5cm) square
- Walnut or cherry, ½" (1.3 cm) thick: 6½" (16.5cm) square
- Basswood, ¾" (1.9cm) thick: approx. 2" x 18" (5.1cm x 45.7cm)
- Pencil
- Wood glue
- Sandpaper: assorted grits up to 500
- Clear finish, such as Odie's Oil and natural Danish oil
- Clean cotton cloths

TOOLS

- Saws: table, miter
- Chip carving knife
- Midi-lathe with assorted turning tools
- Ruler: flexible cloth
- Clamps (or vise)

The author used these products for the project. Substitute your choice of brands, tools, and materials as desired.

TURNING AND CARVING

1 **Turn the bowl.** I turn mine until the circumference at the basswood stripe can be split evenly into round numbers when divided by ¾. Measure using a flexible cloth ruler. Once you've achieved the size you want, sand with 150-grit sandpaper, and then sand progressively through the grits until you reach 500. Apply a natural finish of your choice to the portion that will remain uncarved; leave the outside of the basswood stripe unfinished for now. *Note: I typically sand and finish the bowl while it's on the lathe, so I can take advantage of the friction-finish properties of Odie's Oil, my favorite finish for bowls.*

2 **Apply the pattern to the basswood stripe.** When you're ready to carve, lay out a row of squares that is approximately the same width as the basswood stripe. (I say approximately because it's more important that the circumference of the bowl is divided up evenly than that the pattern is made of perfect squares.) Then draw the diagonals by connecting the corners of each square. Use the center point those diagonals created to mark the vertical and horizontal axis of each square. Then secure the bowl with clamps or a vise so it doesn't wiggle loose during carving.

3 **Carve the bowl.** If you're proficient in Swiss-style chip carving, use the layout from Figure 3 in the pattern to begin. If you're a beginner, you might try English-style chip carving, which is my preferred method. If you chose the latter, begin by making relief cuts along the dotted lines in Figure 4. The deepest part of each relief cut will share a point in the center of each inverted pyramid shape, becoming shallower at the edges. Once you've made a relief cut along each of the dotted lines, you can start removing chips as you would with Swiss-style carving. Work through the rest of the three-corner chips, adjusting the bowl position and vise as necessary until the carving is complete.

4 **Finish the bowl.** I don't sand after carving due to the risk of accidentally softening the crisp edges of the cuts. Apply a natural finish to the carved stripe; I like to use a penetrating oil, such as Danish oil, but any finish that won't pool up on the surface will work. Wipe off the excess with a clean cotton cloth and let dry.

Chip Carved Bowl Patterns

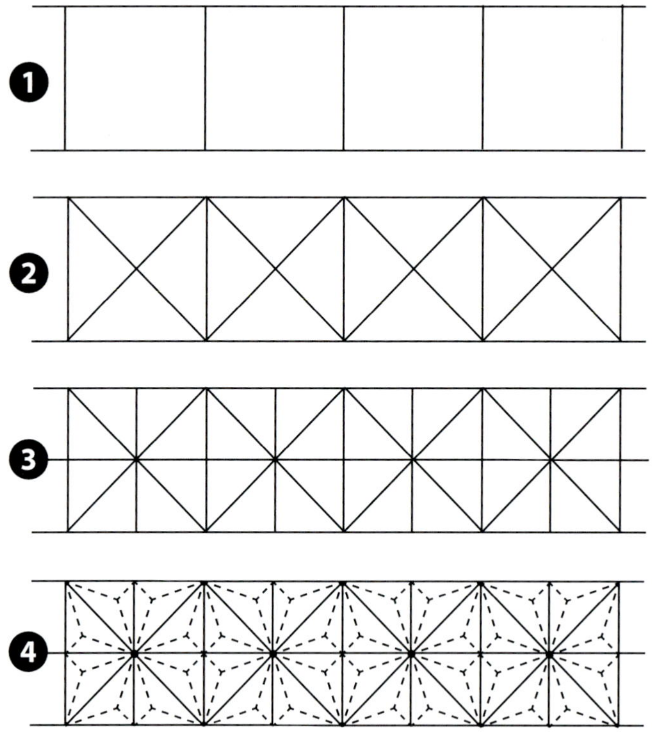

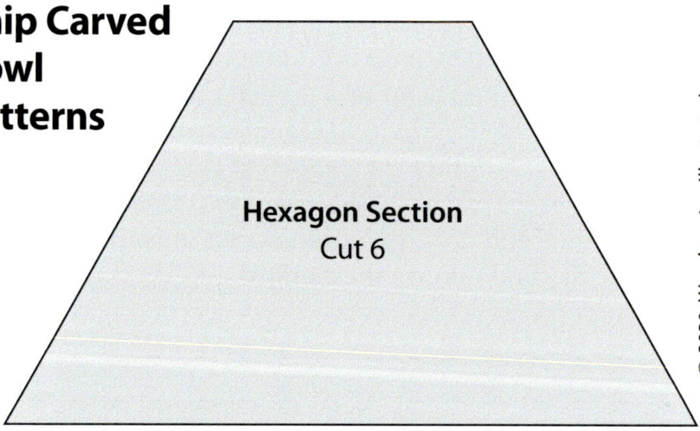

Summery Supernova Coasters

This minimalist chip carving design is chic and perfect for beginners

By Roman Chernikov

If you have avoided chip carving till now because it's too intimidating, then my supernova coasters, inspired by the look of an exploding star, are an ideal first project. In these patterns, I placed the chips farther apart than usual, so no two share the same edge; this virtually eliminates the common mistakes that lead to broken or uneven ridges.

Making the Coasters

Cut the squares to size and sand them smooth using 220-grit sandpaper. Round the edges if desired. Transfer the patterns to the blanks using a hot tool with a laser print or graphite transfer paper. Strop your knife before you begin carving the chips.

I use simple three-corner chips with straight edges to carve the supernovas, which consist of 108 chips each. Refer to the photos to keep track of where the deepest part of the chip should be. Once you've carved the coasters, apply several light coats of acrylic spray finish, letting the piece dry between coats.

materials & **tools**

MATERIALS

- Basswood, at least ¼" (6mm) thick: 4" (10.2cm) square
- Graphite transfer paper (optional)
- Sandpaper: 220-grit
- Finish: clear acrylic spray

TOOLS

- Chip carving knife
- Hot tool (to transfer pattern, optional)

The author used these products for the project. Substitute your choice of brands, tools, and materials as desired.

TIP PRACTICE, PRACTICE, PRACTICE

Making rosettes is the best way to learn carving with the grain, as the chips align with the grain at many different angles. Carve a rosette or two on a practice board before starting your project.

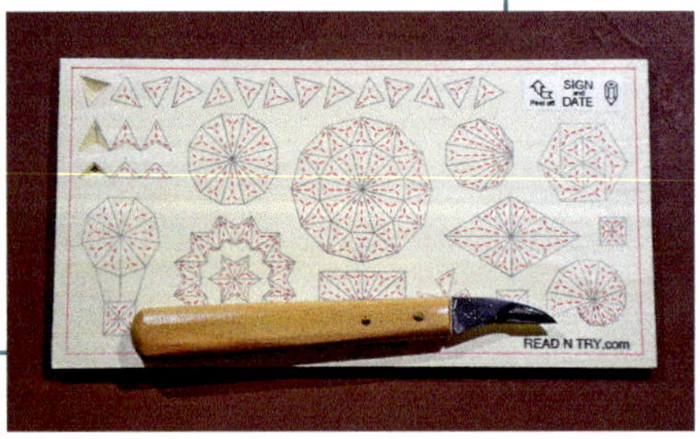

Supernova Coaster Patterns

Coffee Scoop

Simple chip carved design highlights this functional spoon

By Deanna Cadoret

I became interested in carving when I saw everyday wooden items, such as spoons, stools, and jam spreaders, made beautiful by the addition of chip carving. In today's world of mass-produced wooden trinkets, there is little that deserves the effort of chip carving, so I started carving my own items that could then be decorated. Handmade scoops, such as this one, make wonderful gifts, especially when paired with a bag of gourmet coffee.

This scoop is sized to measure out the correct amount of grounds I need for each pot of coffee. If you prefer stronger coffee, make the bowl a bit larger. Test the amount of grounds the scoop will hold as you hollow out the bowl.

Use the same technique to make a set of measuring cups.

The same technique can be used to make measuring cups. To determine if the measuring cups are accurate, fill a store-bought measuring cup with water or rice to the level you want the wooden measuring cup to hold. As you get close to finishing the bowl, pour the contents from the measuring cup into the carved bowl. Continue hollowing the scoop or measuring cup until it holds all of the contents from the measuring cup.

CARVING THE SPOON

1 **Transfer the scoop pattern.** Slide transfer paper under the pattern and trace the top view and side view of the scoop onto the blank. Be sure to include the inside line of the bowl, but do not transfer the chip carving pattern yet.

2 **Rough out the scoop.** Use a band saw to cut away as much waste wood as possible. Cut 1⁄16" (2mm) outside of the pattern lines. You can also use a sharp knife to rough out the scoop.

> **TIP**
> **TRANSFERRING THE PATTERN**
> *Use a non-marking scribing tool to trace the pattern onto the wood. Use a pencil to lightly color the indentations, making them easier to see while carving.*

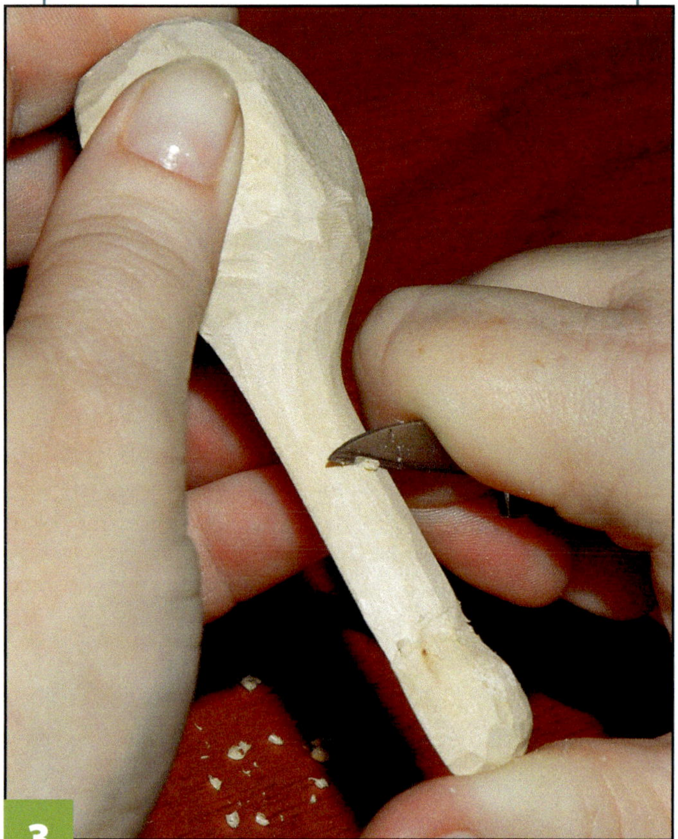

3 **Shape the outside.** Use a knife to remove small amounts of wood from the scoop. Round the bottom of the bowl and carve away the waste outside of the pattern lines. Do not carve away the lines. The lines will be sanded off.

4 **Determine the depth of the bowl.** Drill or carve a ½" (1.3cm)-diameter by ⅝" to ⅞" (1.6cm to 2.2cm)-deep hole in the center of the bowl. I use a ¼" (6mm) #5 gouge to carve the hole. Place the tip of the gouge against the wood just off from the center and spin the gouge around while applying pressure.

5 **Finish carving the bowl.** Use the ¼" (6mm) #5 gouge to carve grooves from the inside border of the bowl to the hole carved in the center. Continue cutting grooves until the outer portion of the bowl is as deep as the center hole.

ADDING THE DECORATION

6 **Transfer the chip carving pattern.** Sand the scoop with 80-grit sandpaper to remove all of the gouge and knife marks. Work your way up through the grits to 600 grit for a smooth finish. The more time you spend sanding, the smoother the finished scoop will be. Transfer the chip carving pattern with a #2 pencil and a very light touch.

7 **Remove the chips.** Cut along the first line with a chip carving knife. Angle the knife so the deepest part of the cut will be in the center of the triangle. Make the two additional cuts. Maintain the same angle on the knife so all three cuts intersect in the center of the triangle. Use the same technique to carve all of the remaining chips.

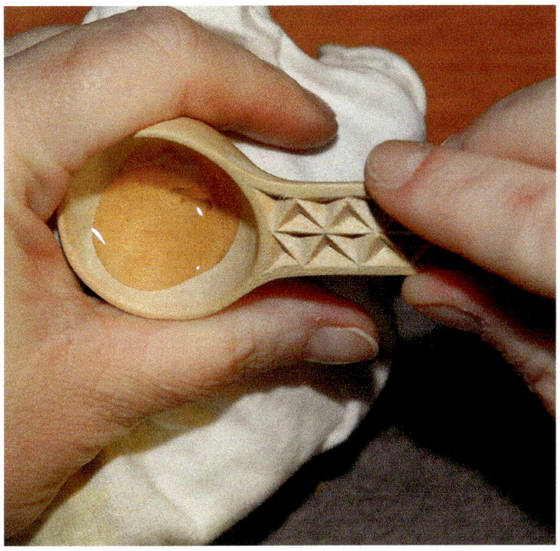

Applying the Finish

Pour about ½ teaspoon of walnut oil into the bowl and rotate the scoop gently to coat the entire inside of the bowl. Pour the excess oil out. Drip a small amount of oil onto the end of the handle and hold the scoop at a gentle incline so the oil fills each chip. Add more oil as needed. Use your finger to apply oil to the back of the scoop. Apply two to three coats of oil, allowing each coat to dry for 24 hours before applying the next coat.

For a deep-penetrating finish, place the scoop and ¼ cup of walnut oil into a plastic resealable bag. Remove as much air as possible and seal the bag. Turn the bag every day for three days. The oil will soak deep into the wood, bringing out the grain, and the oil can be saved for another project.

Store the scoop in coffee grounds. The oils from the coffee will slowly color the scoop.

materials & **tools**

MATERIALS

- Wood, 1" (2.5cm) thick: 1¾" x 4" (4.5cm x 10.2cm)
- Transfer paper
- Sandpaper: assorted grits up to 600
- Plastic reusable bag
- Walnut oil or food-safe finish of choice

TOOLS

- Band saw
- Chip carving knife
- #2 pencil
- #5 gouge: ¼" (6mm)
- Small chip carving knife
- Marking instruments

The author used these products for the project. Substitute your choice of brands, tools, and materials as desired.

Coffee Scoop Pattern

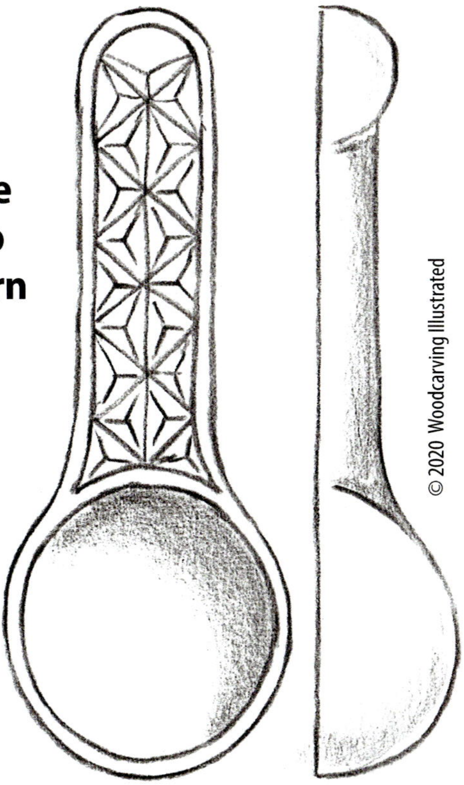

Flower Ornament

Break out of the mold with this organic ornament

By Wayne Barton

Chip carved ornaments are usually based on geometric figures. However, I decided to branch out and make an ornament with a more positive image and organic style. You can display the ornament alone, attach it to the top of a box, or even carve several to decorate a mantel or door frame.

Carving the Flower

Transfer the pattern to the wood with graphite paper. I always advise transferring the pattern with graphite paper rather than gluing the pattern. This way you can see if you are removing or cracking away wood that isn't supposed to be removed.

As you carve the flower, hold the blade at approximately a 65° angle to the wood. When making tight or small curved cuts, raise the angled blade up so it's more on its tip, reducing the amount of metal in the wood. Don't cut deeper than necessary to remove the chips. Keep the "vein" lines narrow so they don't overpower the carving. If desired, add a scalloped border on the back side of the ornament.

Finishing the Flower

Spray both sides of the ornament with three coats of polyurethane, such as Minwax. If desired, paint the outer edge and add a message on the back. Apply a light brown finishing wax, such as Briwax, to both sides of the ornament to emphasize the carved areas while preserving a natural appearance.

Flower Ornament Pattern

NOTE: The diameter of this ornament is 4", but the actual carving is set ¼" inside the outside diameter.

materials & **tools**

MATERIALS

- Basswood, ⅜" (1cm) thick: 5" (12.7cm) square
- Graphite transfer paper
- Spray polyurethane, such as Minwax
- Paint (optional)
- Colored wax, such as Briwax: light brown

The author used these products for the project. Substitute your choice of brands, tools, and materials as desired.

TOOLS

- Chip carving knife

SPECIAL SOURCES

This carving can be completed entirely with two Premier chip carving knives, available from the Alpine School of Wood Carving, chipcarving.com.

Bethlehem Star Hanging

Adorn your home with this stellar chip carved design

By Marty Leenhouts

For this design, I wanted to incorporate long, graceful lines that mimic a star's rays. You'll need to make several small, precise cuts to achieve that look, but the result is stunning. Use the star to top your tree or hang it elsewhere in the house—either way, it's an instant conversation piece.

Prepping and Carving

Photocopy the pattern and use graphite paper to trace it onto the blank. Alternatively, secure a laser copy or photocopy of the pattern facedown and use a heated tool, such as the Pattern Transfer Tool (see Special Sources, below), to transfer the image to the wood. Cut the star on a band saw or scroll saw.

Carve the central flower and diamonds. Then add the decorative details around the flower. Many of the chips can be removed with two or three cuts. Keep the joint of your thumb on the thumb notch and try to visualize the point of your knife reaching the center of each chip. When the cuts meet, the chip will pop out. Remove all leftover pattern lines (I use a Tombow Sand Eraser). Be especially careful around the delicate side tips of the star, as they can easily break.

Finishing

You can finish the star in a number of ways. I chose a natural look. The easiest finish can be completed, beginning-to-end, in less than two hours. Spray two coats of satin lacquer or clear matte acrylic finish on the surface of the carving. Allow 30 minutes of dry time between coats. Lightly sand with 220-grit sandpaper, vacuum off the dust, and spray on a final coat.

If you do wish to add color to the star, carefully brush a gel stain into the recessed areas after your clear finish has dried. Wipe off any excess from the surface with a cotton cloth and let dry overnight. Apply more gel stain as needed; I add a final clear topcoat for a consistent finish.

Display as desired. If your star will be a wall piece, attach a D-ring hanger to the back. To make a unique tree topper, attach an alligator clip (available at craft stores) to the back of the star with cyanoacrylate (CA) glue. Clip the star to the top of your tree for all to see!

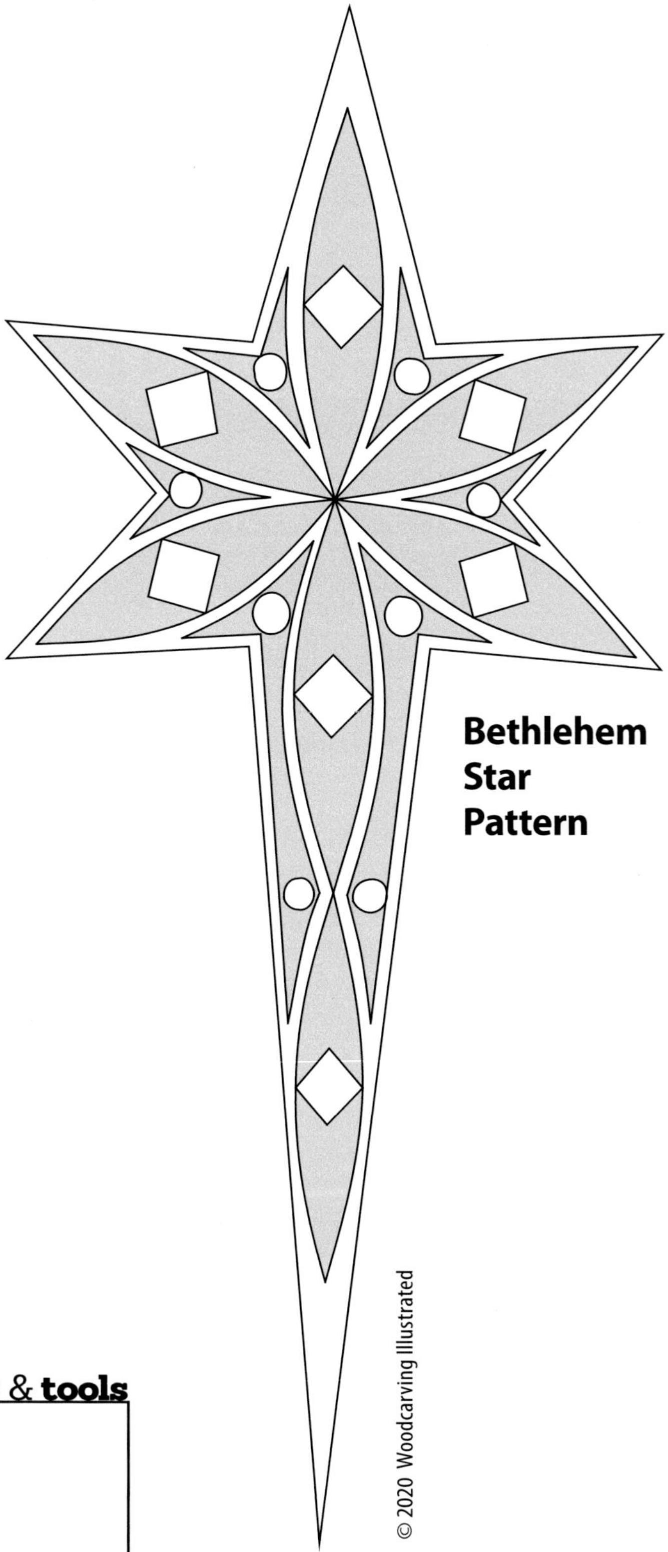

Bethlehem Star Pattern

materials & **tools**

MATERIALS

- Basswood, 3/8" (1cm) thick: 3½" x 8" (8.9cm x 20.3cm)
- Graphite paper
- Pencil
- Sandpaper: 220-grit
- Tombow Sand Eraser (optional)
- Finish: satin spray lacquer or clear matte acrylic
- Gel stain (optional)
- Cotton cloth (optional)
- D-ring hanger (optional)
- Alligator clip (optional)
- Cyanoacrylate (CA) glue (optional)

TOOLS

- Scroll saw or band saw
- Chip carving knife, such as a diamond modified knife
- Pattern transfer tool (optional)
- Vacuum
- Paintbrush (optional)

The author used these products for the project. Substitute your choice of brands, tools, and materials as desired.

SPECIAL SOURCES

A Pattern Transfer Tool and diamond modified knife are available from MyChipCarving.com.

Holly Napkin Holder

Chip carve this simple design to dress up any holiday table

By Marty Leenhouts

This napkin holder is functional and beautiful. It will add a nice touch to your family get-togethers. Adding color makes it truly eye-catching and is sure to generate some conversation about your carving.

Getting Started

Start by transferring the pattern to the top. I use a Pattern Transfer Tool (see Special Sources on page 41) with a fresh laser copy for this first step. You could also use graphite paper to transfer the pattern to the blank. This is a positive image carving, which means you will carve away the dark background areas while the holly leaves and berries remain flush with the surface.

Carving and Painting

- When you don't know how to carve a particular part of the pattern, apply it to a practice board. Work out these challenges on a practice board, and then your confidence will soar when you make the same cuts on your final project.
- Concentrate on keeping the same angle on all cuts. As a chip gets wider, increase the depth of the knife and maintain the same angle.
- Use a smaller knife to make the tight, deep, curved cuts. I use a knife with less metal on the spine, such as my Modified Chip Carving Knife (see Special Sources), which makes it easier to carve a smooth, chatter-free curve. Strop the knife regularly to maintain a sharp edge.
- To avoid chipping off the sharp tips of the holly leaves, always make the second cut from the tip down. Carving from the tip down will preserve these sharp, delicate areas. Making the second cut toward the tip increases the chances that the tip of the holly leaf will chip off.
- Paint the holly leaves and berries in natural, authentic colors. I mix acrylic paints to achieve these results. Use a mixing chart and make adjustments as needed until the colors look just right.
- If you need more help carving and finishing this project, watch the video on my website, MyChipCarving.com. Seeing how it's done can make all the difference.

Holly Napkin Holder Measured Drawings

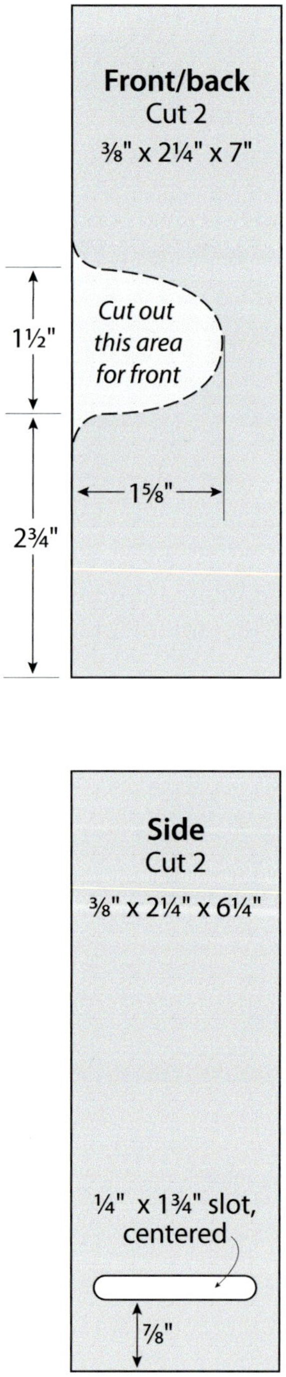

Holly Napkin Holder Assembly Drawing

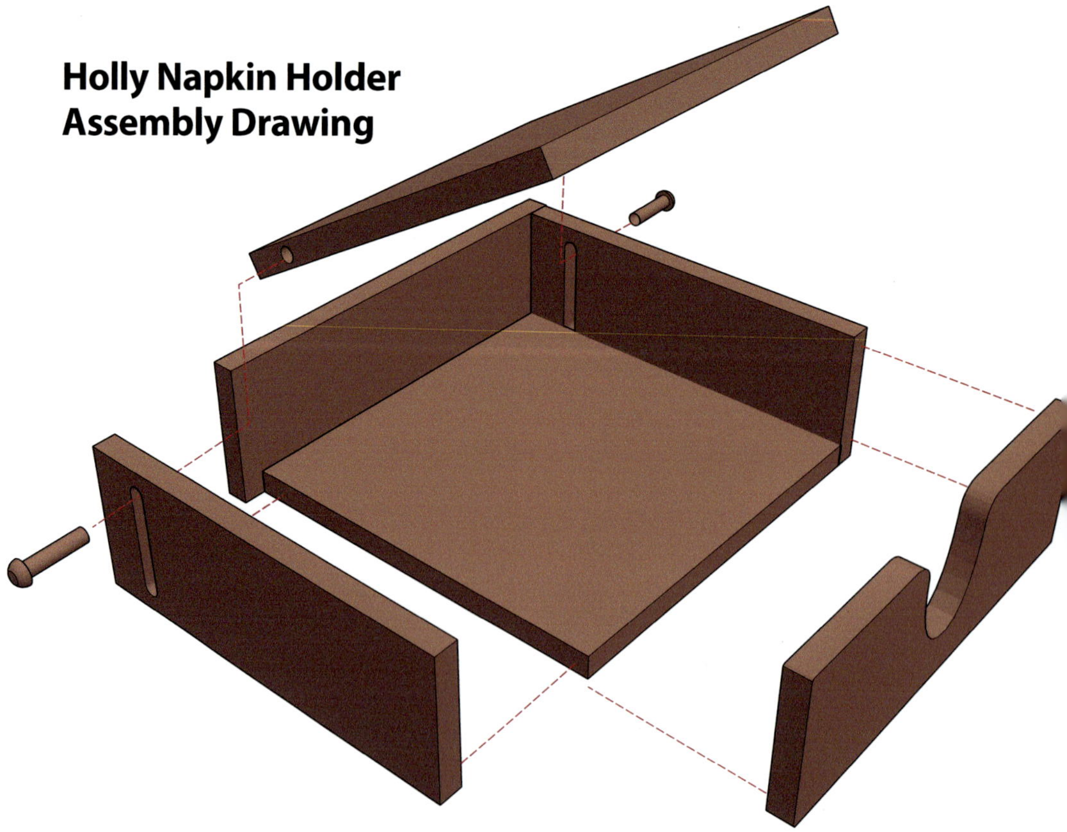

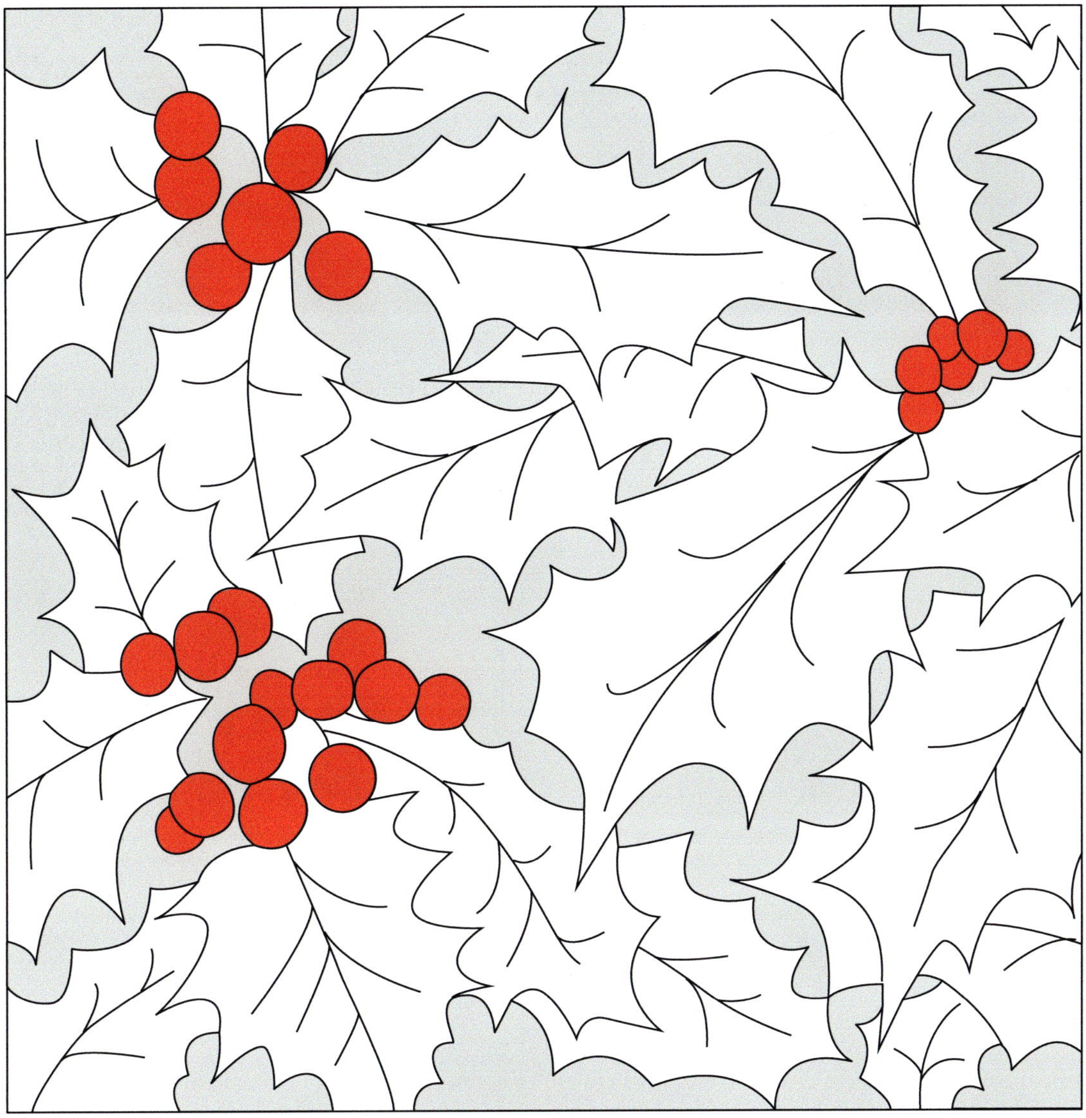

Holly Napkin Holder Pattern

materials & **tools**

MATERIALS

- Basswood, 3/8" (1cm) thick: 2 each, front/back, 2¼" x 7" (5.7cm x 17.8cm); 2 each, sides, 2¼" x 6¼" (5.7cm x 15.9cm); top, 6¼" (15.9cm) square
- Baltic birch plywood, 1/8" (3mm) thick: bottom, 6¼" (15.9cm) square
- Axle pegs: 2 each 3/16" (5mm)-dia.
- Wood glue
- Acrylic paint: brown, green, red
- Graphite paper (optional)

The author used these products for the project. Substitute your choice of brands, tools, and materials as desired

TOOLS

- Chip carving knife
- Pattern transfer tool (optional)
- Drill with bits: assorted small
- Paintbrushes: assorted

SPECIAL SOURCES

A preassembled napkin holder is available for $17.95 plus S&H. The modified chip carving knife is available for $29.95. The Pattern Transfer Tool is available for $19.95. Call 866-444-6996 or visit MyChipCarving.com for more details.

Snowflake Baubles

Mix and match designs to create dozens of easy ornaments

By Gary MacKay

These designs are easy to cut and carve. I cut the snowflakes on a scroll saw, but you could also carve the designs on round or square blanks. Mix and match the designs to create sets of unique ornaments.

Making the Ornaments

Attach the patterns to the basswood with spray adhesive. Cut the perimeter. You can carve directly through the paper, but for more accurate cuts, draw the patterns directly onto the wood. Soak the patterns with mineral spirits to remove them, and wipe off any excess adhesive with a rag soaked in mineral spirits. Sand carefully with 220-grit sandpaper to remove any fuzzies, making sure to not sand off the sharp corners of the chips. Apply a clear spray finish.

Troubleshooting Your Chips

A few things can go wrong when you chip carve. Here are a few examples of bad chips and how to prevent them.

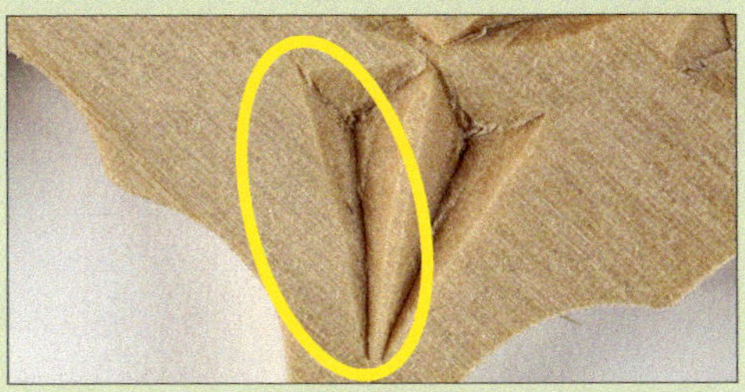

Wavy edges like this appear for three reasons: a dull knife, starting and stopping repeatedly while cutting, or going back to try to clean up the cuts. Remember to strop often, position your hand so you can complete each cut in one smooth movement, and make sure any cuts you make to clean up the edges of the chip are at the same angle as the first cuts.

Fuzzy bits of wood left in the bottom of the chips appear when your cuts do not meet. Some larger chips require you to remove smaller chips first, but whenever possible, cut deep enough to free the chips the first time. If you do need to make multiple cuts, make sure you cut at the same angle. When in doubt, make your cut deeper to make sure you free the chip.

Sometimes you want a rounded corner, but in most cases, chip carving depends on uniform sharp corners. To carve sharp corners, make sure the cuts you use to free the chip meet exactly. If a chip doesn't pop out cleanly, chances are the corners will suffer.

Snowflake Ornament Patterns

Snowflake Ornament Patterns

Snowflake Ornament Patterns

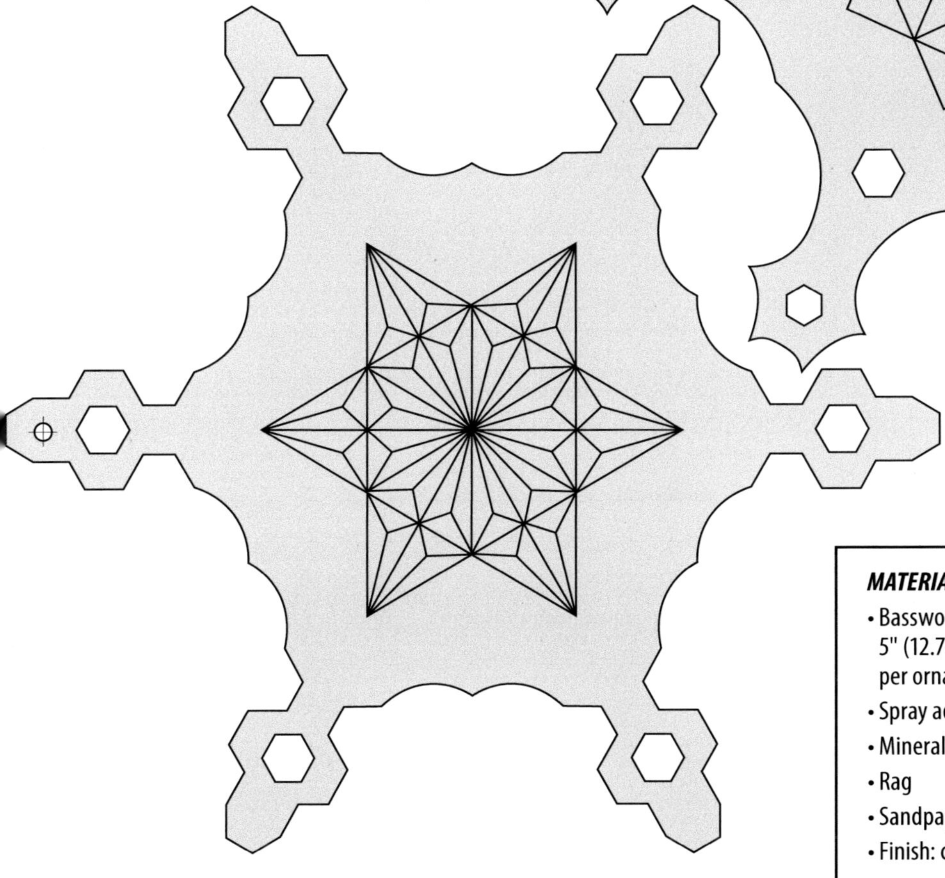

materials & **tools**

MATERIALS

- Basswood ¼" (6mm) thick: 5" (12.7cm) square, per ornament
- Spray adhesive
- Mineral spirits
- Rag
- Sandpaper: 220-grit
- Finish: clear spray

TOOLS

- Scroll saw with blades: #5 reverse-tooth
- Drill with bit: 3⁄32" (2.5mm)-dia. twist
- Chip carving knife

The author used these products for the project. Substitute your choice of brands, tools, and materials as desired.

Snowflake Ornament Patterns

Old-Fashioned Sleds

Slide into winter with these clean, geometric decorations

By Charlene Lynum

Having grown up in the Midwest, I have many fond memories of gliding downhill with my brothers, with the snow in our faces and our cheeks pink from the cold. Those days inspired these patterns using simple two- and three-corner chips that don't take days to master and look fantastic when they're complete.

Getting Started

Sand the blank with 220-grit sandpaper and attach the patterns; I ironed a laser copy on using a pattern transfer tool, but you can trace the designs on with graphite paper and a pencil, if desired. Be sure to place the pattern on the outward facing side of both runners. Orient the grain vertically along the length of the sled and runners. Cut the sled body with a scroll saw; I like to use a #5 reverse-tooth blade so I get a smooth cut on both the bottom and top of the project. (This reduces the amount of sanding needed.) I recommend stack-cutting the pieces for the runners so they're identical. Secure the stack with double-faced tape. Then drill the ⅛" (3mm)-dia. hole for the dowel while they're still stacked so the holes line up, and cut the runners.

Carving, Assembling, and Finishing

Carve the sled and runner designs. Always make sure to angle your blade so the deepest point coincides with the center of each chip. To assemble the sleds, slide the runners on the dowel with the carved sides out. Place a small amount of wood glue on each end of the dowel, and then slide a runner out to each end of the dowel, using the 1" (2.5cm) scrap spacer for correct spacing. Make sure the runners sit flat on the table. You may need to twist them on the dowel to make this happen, so adjust them before the glue dries.

Place the carved sled top on a solid surface with the carved side down. Place a very small ribbon of glue on the top edge of both runners. Center the runners on the bottom side of the sled top. Make sure the top of the runners (doweled end) and the top of the sled (the side that's curved outward) are on the same end. Remove any squeeze-out with a clean paper towel. Make sure that your spacer doesn't get glued to the sled, as you will discard it later. Place a small weight (e.g. can of soup) on thc runners and allow to dry. Once the assembly has dried, remove the spacer. Apply a finish and display as desired; I used clear satin polyurethane and hung mine with colored ribbon.

materials & **tools**

MATERIALS

- Basswood, ¼" (6mm) thick: sled top, 1¾" x 3¼" (4.4cm x 8.3cm)
- Basswood, ¼" (6mm) thick: runners, 2 each ¾" x 4⅛" (1.9cm x 10.5cm)
- Scrap wood ¼" (6mm) thick: spacer, 1" x 2" (2.5cm x 5.1cm)
- Wood dowel, ⅛" (3mm)-dia.: 1½" (3.8cm) long
- Pencil (optional)
- Graphite paper (optional)
- Tape: double-faced
- Wood glue
- Sandpaper: 220-grit
- Paper towels
- Finish, such as Minwax clear satin fast-drying polyurethane
- Colored ribbon or string (optional)

TOOLS

- Scroll saw with blades: #5 reverse-tooth
- Drill with bit: ⅛" (3mm)-dia.
- Pattern transfer tool (optional)
- Chip carving knife

The author used these products for the project. Substitute your choice of brands, tools, and materials as desired.

Sled Ornament Patterns

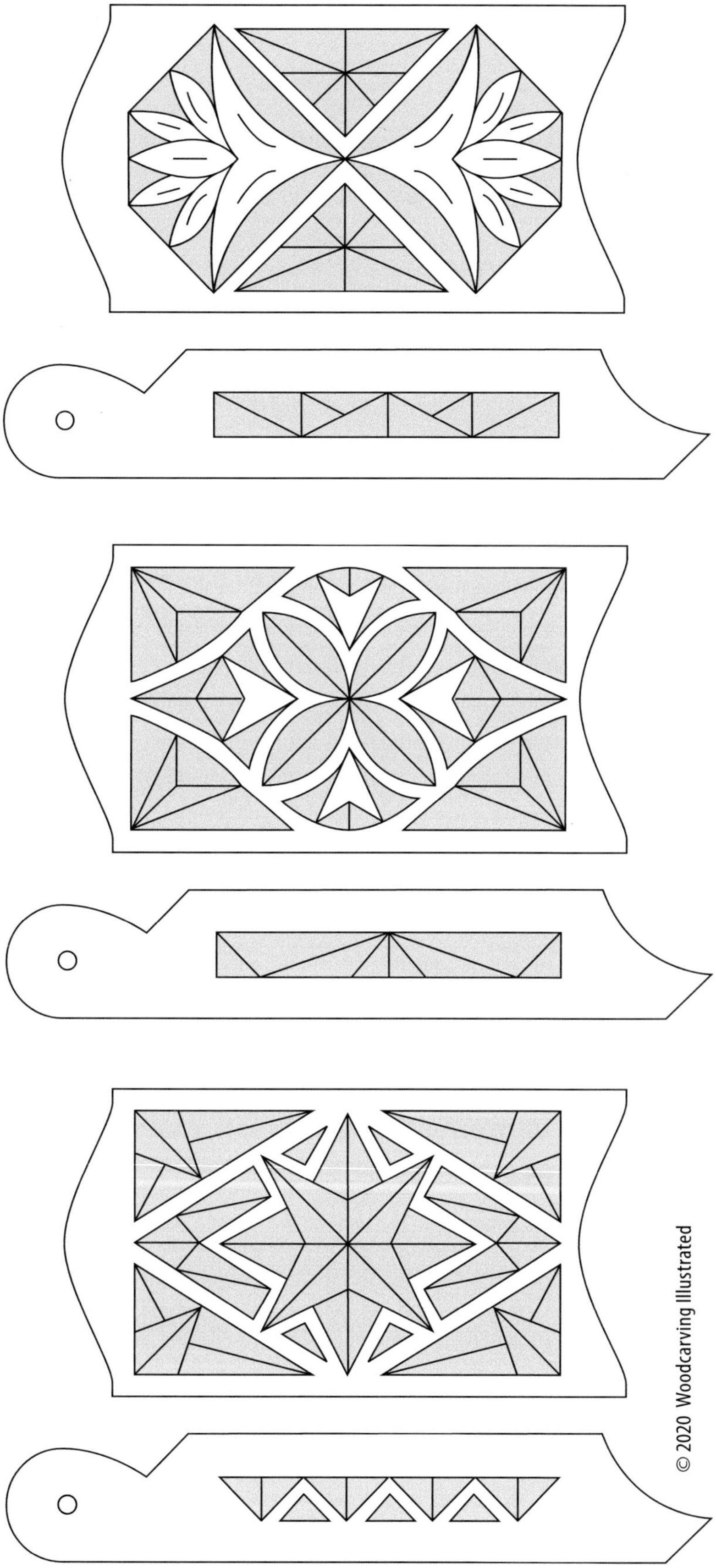